THE ELECTRIC HUMANITIES

THE ELECTRIC HUMANITIES

patterns for teaching
mass media & popular culture
by Don Allen

photography & graphics
by Brent Warren

Geo. A. Pflaum, Publisher, Dayton, Ohio 45402

Library of Congress Catalog Card Number 77-160514
Printed in the United States of America

This book is dedicated to my wife, my family, my friends, my students, my teachers, and everyone else who helped me get it on.

—Don Allen
Winter, 1971

CONTENTS

INDIAN
OCEAN

electric
adj.
1. of or charged with electricity.
2. producing or produced by electricity.
3. operated by electricity.
4. electrifying; exciting.

humanities
n. the branches of learning concerned with human thought and relations; esp. literature, philosophy, etc.

—**Webster's New World Dictionary of the American Language** (Popular Library Pocket-Size Edition)

"It's very fashionable, you know—being young."
—comment of an observer
at a Be-In

"Well, the way I see it, there's a lot more of them than there is of us, so we'd better find out what they're thinkin' . . ."
—one elderly citizen to another,
while observing youth influx
at a Folk-Rock Festival

THE ELECTRIC HUMANITIES

youth myths & hip hypes

We seem to be caught up in what might be termed the "And A Little Child Shall Lead Them" Syndrome. / The popular magazines announce new "Generations" (Love, Drug, Rock, Revolution, etc.) on an almost weekly basis. The "youth market" makes up a major part of the consumer population. In fashion, entertainment, and even politics, youth must be served, youth must be sold.

Convenient myths arise. The predominant myth being that kids are "hip"—that kids know "what's happening." This myth is perpetrated by disc jockeys, admen, and all the various hype artists who make their livings cashing in on kids.

Kids, however, like most of us these days, are in fact often confused, frustrated, and generally messed up. If they were **really** hip, they might well be less confused, less frustrated, and less messed up. If kids were hip, teachers would probably be out of work.

In terms of hip, beads, buckskin, beards, and boots are really beside the point. Hip is a subjective term, hard to define and impossible to measure on an empirical five-point scale of 5) very hip, 4) hipper-than-thou, 3) typically hip, 2) unhip, and 1) plastic. Hip is essentially attitudinal.

"Whatever these things called 'beatniks' and 'hippies' originally were, or still are, may have nothing to do with what **Time, Esquire, Cheeta,** CBSNBCABC, Broadway comedy, and Hollywood have decided to make of them."

—Theodore Roszak,
The Making of a Counter Culture

"Young people are looking for a formula for putting on the universe—**participation mystique.** They do not look for detached patterns—for ways of relating themselves to the world, a la nineteenth century."

—Marshall McLuhan,
The Medium is the Massage

For our purposes, let us define "hip" as follows:

hip adj. (<old American slang **hep**)
1. sensitive to the total environment.
2. knowledgeable about oneself and oneself in relation to others.
3. having an awareness of changes within one's milieu and the ability to use the awareness to understand and deal with the changes.
4. perceptive.

Hip has virtually nothing to do with age, **Teen** magazine **et al.** to the contrary. For example, Marshall McLuhan, Buckminster Fuller, Alan Watts, Kurt Vonnegut, Jr., and Stanley Kubrick are all hip—not a teenager in the bunch.

The purpose of the Electric Humanities is to make kids hip.

education & the other education

In a sense, making people hip should be the purpose of all education. But education, by and large, "looks at the present through a rear-view mirror" (as McLuhan would say). The 19th century is alive and well in the 20th century American schools, as has been frequently pointed out with little noticeable effect.

However, for today's kids, there is a 20th century education available. The Other Education comes on at 24 frames-per-second or at 33-1/3 revolutions-per-minute, or even instantaneously. The Other Education encompasses

"Today in our cities, most learning occurs outside the classroom. The sheer quantity of information conveyed by press-magazines-film-TV-radio far exceeds the quantity of information conveyed by school instruction and texts. This challenge has destroyed the monopoly of the book as a teaching aid and cracked the very walls of classroom so suddenly that we're confused, baffled."

—McLuhan, "Classroom Without Walls" in **Explorations in Communications**

"Aunt Margaret and Uncle Henry took their school days with some seriousness because they knew that what was going on in the schoolroom was related to what was going on outside. This relation is no longer possible in our electric environment which makes the 'outside' information level far higher—and far more exciting—than the information level of the present schoolroom. The present educational establishment, with its factory-like setups, seems bizarre to many young people because they are growing up in a world where all data and events appear integrally related."

—R. Buckminster Fuller, **I Seem To Be a Verb**

fact and fiction, history and fantasy, comedy and tragedy, art and kitsch, sociology, psychology, philosophy, mythology, and the entire enchilada. The Other Education is the mass media, and that is what the Electric Humanities is all about.

electric humanities: shed a little light

The Electric Humanities is an attempt to bring together the Other Education and the classroom version of education. The Electric Humanities is interdisciplinary and non-academic. The Electric Humanities is an English course, a social studies course, an art course, and not a course at all. The Electric Humanities is learning to look and see, learning to listen and hear, learning to think and feel, learning how to learn.

The concept of the Electric Humanities began as a film course, movies having received their cultural credentials in recent years; but as John Culkin has said, "All the media have something to offer. All the media should be taught in the schools." A reasonable suggestion, considering the pervasive influence of TV, radio, film, recorded music, and the press as opposed to, say, the poetry of James Russell Lowell or the presidency of Millard Fillmore.

The concept of the Electric Humanities was eventually expanded to include even the less respectable media, all of which are a part of American popular culture which, in itself, warrants study.

"What is the business of the schools? To create eager consumers? To transmit the dead ideas, values, metaphors, and information of three minutes ago? To create smoothly functioning bureaucrats? **These** aims are truly subversive since they undermine our chances of surviving as a viable, democratic society. And they do their work in the name of convention and standard practice. We would like to see the schools go into the anti-entropy business. Now, that is subversive, too. But the purpose is to subvert attitudes, beliefs, and assumptions that foster chaos and uselessness."

—Neil Postman & Charles Weingartner, **Teaching as a Subversive Activity**

"Lavishing vast and increasing amounts of time, energy, and money, we assiduously prepare our students for a world that no longer exists. We have created an educational system that in truth interrupts the student's education."

—R. Buckminster Fuller, **I Seem To Be a Verb**

The significance of the popular arts may be temporal, but they are of crucial importance NOW. And NOW is what kids are most interested in. NOW gives us the best starting point for the study of THEN and WHEN.

An avant-garde in education is practically a contradiction in terms. In those instances where media study is taught at all, it is probably misused and abused as often as not. Fitting it into the framework of the traditional school is tantamount to the old trick of inserting the round peg in the square hole. In the end, if it endures, it is as often as an exotic novelty, an educational "frill."

Those of us involved may see ourselves as revolutionary, while our more conservative colleagues tend to view us as eccentrics. And the same old system, shakily supporting some shadowy status quo, plods on.

Another problem is the aforementioned matter of youth myths & hip hypes. In the areas contained within the Electric Humanities spectrum, many teachers seem to feel incriminated by the so-called "generation gap." Certainly, it is as dangerous to generalize about teachers as a group as it is to generalize about kids. There are hip teachers, both over and under the borderline age of 30. Such

"In this violently upsetting social situation, many teachers naturally view the offerings of the new media as entertainment rather than education. But this carries no conviction to the student."

—McLuhan,
"Classroom Without Walls"

"One must make certain assumptions in order to get on with one's work. Therefore, let us assume that America values its youth, that our community leaders want our youth to know reality and not just fantasy, and that our teachers do not fear youth and their need to know about the world they live in."

—Postman & Weingartner,
Teaching as a Subversive Activity

"Teacher have seldom felt more alienated from the kids; yet it has seldom been easier to make contact with their world. We communicate with people by having something in common with them. One thing we can all have in common is the mass media."

—John M. Culkin, "I was a Teen-Age Movie Teacher" in **The Saturday Review** (July, 1966) superficial dichotomies and stereotypes as over-30/under-30, teacher/student, adult/kid, unhip/hip only serve to build barricades between people, limit learning, and confound communication. We are all in this thing together.

Some will hold the view that kids, having grown up with the mass media, are more conversant in the special languages the media employ. This is not necessarily the case. To be inured to something doesn't necessarily imply insight. That kids are responsive to the media doesn't necessarily indicate inherent abilities to analyze and understand.

Teachers, on the other hand, by virtue of being older than their kids, have supposedly paid some dues—learned a little more by living longer, developed their critical faculties. Somewhere between the kids' enthusiastic response and the teacher's experienced, analytical eye must lie a delicate balance where productive dialogue can begin.

For the most part, the media are a mystery to us all. But such a mega-mystery deserves some scrutiny. Sociological studies to determine alleged effects of mass media are generally inconclusive, but each of us, as an individual, can cite certain effects on the personal level. The Electric Humanities provides an opportunity to do just that.

"I am at a loss to know where, besides among these dissenting young people and their heirs of the next few generations, the radical discontent and innovation can be found that might transform this disoriented civilization of ours into something a human being can identify as home."

—Theodore Roszak,
The Making of a Counter Culture

comes the revolution

There is much badinage, these days, about REVOLUTION(!). The talk is often in the future tense, when, in fact, it should be in the past and present tenses. The Revolution has been on for at least a decade, so if you just came in, you're late.

The nature of the real revolution is not violent/political, but non-violent/cultural, and it is being brought off by a small but growing band of conspirators, scarcely suspect as they set about subverting America's youth with creeping honesty and idealism. Some of these cultural guerillas are writers. Some are the artists. Some are filmmakers. Some are even teachers.

They wage their own special kind of warfare in the "battle for men's hearts and minds" by defining our problems, by showing us our possibilities, and by propagandizing for humanistic changes in values and attitudes on the part of the individual and society at large.

Long after the paranoia and polarization have passed, long after the hue and cry have died away, the victory will go to the young. As always, they inherit the earth. The question is, what will they do with it once it is theirs? The answer will be determined by the outcome of the cultural revolution.

"It is a matter of the greatest urgency that our educational institutions realize that we now have civil war among these environments created by media other than the printed word. The classroom is now in a vital struggle for survival with the immensely persuasive 'outside' world created by new informational media."

—McLuhan, **The Medium is the Massage**

education as a mass medium

The Revolution works in weird ways its wonders to perform. It works mostly through the mass media. Education is a massive mass medium, unique in that it is the only medium with the capability of instant feedback. It can only be turned off by dropping out (The expression should have been, "Tune Out, Turn Off, Drop Out"). Why this terrific medium is not used more effectively is puzzling indeed.

One major difference between the old education and the other education is that the latter is generally entertaining, while the former is frequently dull, boring, and lifeless. Why is that?

If entertainment can function as education, why not vice-versa?

Most of us will spend endless hours with friends discussing movies, music, and the various media products, and then in the classroom, revert to the old 19th-century lecture approach to 19th-century material. Not that there is nothing worthwhile in the 19th century and previous centuries, but again, the importance lies in how it has to do with now. It is natural, I suppose, to feel more comfortable with that which is over and done with, but unless we can use the past to probe the present, we are merely involved in a pedantic pastime. And, unless we begin to probe the present and the future, we many be over and done with.

"To have great poets there must be great audiences."

—Walt Whitman

patterns for probing

Lest I wax too ecstatic about masspop, let me acknowledge that, of course, there is much in it that is trite, banal, vulgar, and otherwise worthless. The best and the worst, however, are both reflections of the society from which they come.

An integral function of the Electric Humanities is the development of a talent for what Postman & Weingartner call "Crap Detecting"—demythologyzing, making important distinctions between images and realities.

What is presented throughout this book is, by no means, a step-by-step study guide for this is not so much a "How To" book as it is a "What To" or perhaps a "Why To" book. The purpose is to promote creative, individualized approaches to education. "Each child is different" (as they used to say in teachers' college), and each school is different. There is no valid masterplan for the Electric Humanities. Herein, you will find patterns—concepts for customization according to your own particular needs.

For instance, I teach the Electric Humanities in a "target area" (read: ghetto) school, and my kids are much more apt to be into motorcycle movies and the sounds of the Shangri-Las than, say, the films of Federico Fellini or the music of Frank Zappa. Wherever your kids are at is the best place to begin. Start there. You can learn a lot from them. They can learn a lot from each other. Maybe, they'll even learn something from you.

"I sing the body electric,
The armies of those I love engirth me
and I engirth them,
They will not let me off till I go with them,
respond to them,
And discorrupt them, and charge them full with
the charge of the soul . . ."
—Walt Whitman

The trick is to teach the total environment.
If it exists, explore it.
Everything is everything and, in the end,
it all comes back to basics.
You can get where you're going from anywhere,
but always remember to bring it all back home.

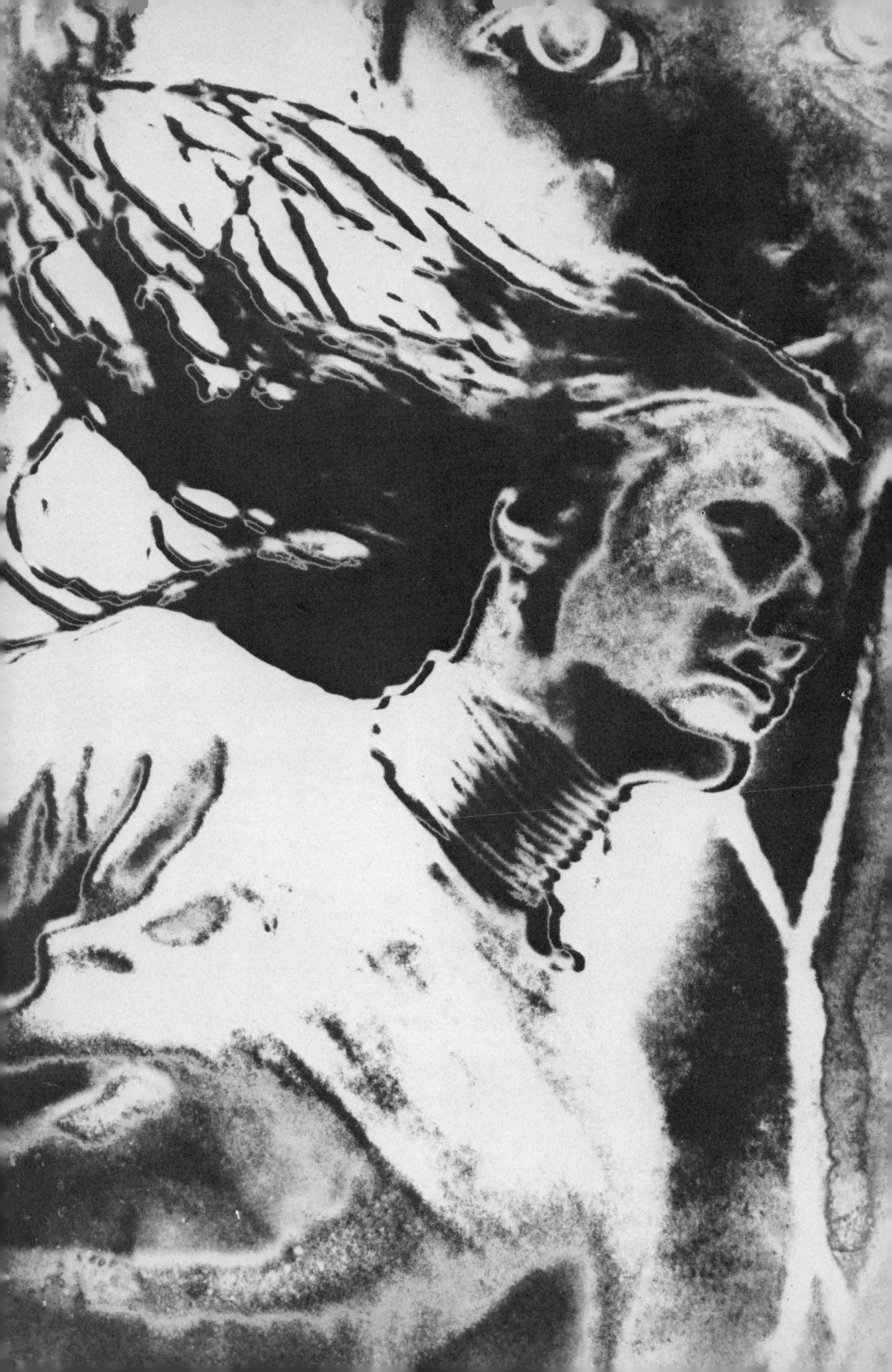

THE ELECTRIC ENVIRONMENT

Look around . . . Listen . . .

The day begins. Your AM/FM clock radio wakes you with a five-minute summary of all the news of the world that has taken place since the last five-minute news summary you heard before you dozed off the night before, followed by a minute of ad jingles, followed by three minutes of number twenty-two on this week's Top Forty, followed by the patter of a disc jockey who bemoans the early hour, followed by a traffic report relayed from an airborne helicopter hovering over the congested arteries of the city freeway, followed by number seventeen . . .

Over your coffee, you recap the news by reading the headlines of the morning paper; and the evening TV schedule which announces that the President of the United States will be appearing in your living room tonight to discuss America's foreign policy; and the entertainment pages which advertise the openings of five new films this week, including an Italian western, a Super-Panavision 150 recreation of the decline and fall of the Roman Empire, an X-rated underground attack on the Establishment, a revival of a Walt Disney kiddie classic, and the grande prix winner at the Cannes Film Festival—a Swedish cinematic study of the silence of God; and you chuckle briefly at Charlie Brown's inability to cope with his kite.

"What we have here is a failure to communicate."
—Strother Martin in
COOL HAND LUKE

"At this 'somewhere/somewhen' you are immersed in a great ocean of other happenings. The interactions between the 'happening' that is you and the 'happenings' that are not you, are the raw, basic stuff we try to communicate about."
—Don Fabun,
Communications (Kaiser Aluminum News)

"So even when we are looking at 'the same thing'—that is, in the same direction and from exactly the same spot—we still do not necessarily experience it the same way (A good example is the quite different reactions people get from watching the same motion picture)."
—Fabun, **Communications**

It is a day like all days, "filled with those events that alter and illuminate our lives."

This, then, is our Electric Environment, the cyclotron through which we're passed, bombarded with high-speed electro-information, and surely somehow transformed. To the technician, it's technology. To most of us, it's magic. It's called "communication."

communication, personal

We each make our own mental movie: THE CONTINUING SAGA OF **(your name).**

A baby is born—Lights! Camera! Action! Immediately, his movie goes into production. He will write the screenplay, cast the characters, direct the action, and edit the rushes for about three score years and ten. But he never appears in his own movie, despite the fact that he is the leading man, around whom the entire plot revolves. An old man dies—Fade out . . . Bring up title: THE END.

I am a camera. You are a camera. Perhaps, I am in your movie. Perhaps, you are in mine. Perhaps, a film festival is in order. We could all share our scenarios.

This movie metaphor points out some problems concerning perception. The purpose of discussing perception is that it is a fundamental factor of communication, and the fundamentals of communication seem to be a good place to begin.

"It is sometimes useful to think of human communications as 'transactions'. In the sense we mean here, a transaction involves the interaction of the observer and what he observes. This can take place between ourselves and the world-outside-our-skin. Or it can take place between two or more human beings. The transaction may be an exchange of specially-created visual events, such as written words, works of art, photographs, charts, equations, etc., or in the form of spoken symbols as in ordinary conversation, speeches, songs and music. Whatever the symbolization, the basic ingredients of the transaction are the same.

"These transactions may include:
Something taken in . . .
Something transformed . . .
Something retained . . .
Something created . . .
Something transmitted . . ."

—Fabun, **Communications**

Much is made today of the "lack of communication" as a primal cause for just about everything from individual alienation to international war. Ironically, our facilities for communicating have never been as extensive as they are today. Still, the technological tools of communication are virtually wasted if the communicator isn't sure about what he wants to say, or if the party he addresses is unprepared to receive his message. Whatever faults afflict our abilities to communicate, it seems safe to assume that they occur more frequently at the human level than they do in the mechanics of our media.

For this reason, perhaps we should preface our investigation of mass communication with a brief review of communications rules a la English class.

If nothing else, a grasp of the basic concept of the "communications loop" is imperative:

Somewhere within this simple circle, our communication breakdowns usually originate.

The communications loop is central to all subsequent phases of the Electric Humanities. Throughout the survey, we shall be considering the various media creators as "Senders" and ourselves as "Receivers." Our "Responses" to the "Messages" are the content of the course.

"We shouldn't have too many problems if we can keep a few things in mind:

1. At best, our perception and knowledge of what we can talk about is limited and fragmentary . . .
2. Whenever we talk about something, we are talking about something that happened inside of us, not something outside of us . . .
3. What happened inside of us did not necessarily happen the same way inside someone else . . .
4. Common words do not in themselves have meaning; only the people who use them have meanings . . ."

—Fabun, **Communications**

Surveying communications, including the related studies of psychology, linguistics, semantics, symbology, et al., is obviously an impossible and impractical undertaking for one phase of a general survey of mass media and popular culture, but at least, a general review/over-view of the basic principles is in order before proceeding further.

Illustrations of the principles are readily available by merely dissecting any normal conversation. Just watch for gross generalizations, misconstrued meanings, inadequate observations, fallacious "facts," subjective "objectivity," unwarranted assumptions, implication by inflection and intonation, categorical stereotypes, and the usual standard sins. By constantly questioning the random remarks of others, one can easily develop the power to make men mad. And our aim, of course, is to clarify communication, not to bring it to a hostile halt. Take care.

Numerous illustrative games can be developed simply by short-circuiting the communications loop. An obvious example is the old party trick of passing a whispered sentence around among a group, and comparing what emerges with the original. Or, try cutting off the feedback (e.g. one person gives verbal instructions to another who cannot respond with questions for clarification). Or, attempt a few experiments in non-verbal communication (e.g. "Charades"). Apply your imagination.

We are, after all, involved in similar communications games constantly, and an awareness of that fact is an important first step toward understanding the sound and the fury.

Hello flower
Hello cloud

"The most favorable moment to seize a man and influence him is when he is alone in the mass . . ."

—Jacques Ellul, **Propaganda: The Formation of Men's Attitudes**

"On the whole, however, the similarities between the processes of mass communication and inter-personal communication are far greater than the differences. Mass communications faces the same defenses and must leap the same hurdles: attention, acceptance, interpretation, and storing. It requires the same kinds of contracts between sender and receiver for entertainment and instruction. It must depend upon activating the same kinds of psychological dynamics if it is to persuade."

—William L. Rivers & Wilbur Schramm **Responsibility in Mass Communication**

communications, mass

Having glimpsed the hazards of everyday interpersonal communication, we can quickly conclude that communication **en masse** must be a mess. For now the loop comes unlooped and we have:

SENDER
↓
MESSAGE
↓
RECEIVER

You can't ask Antonioni what he **meant** in his movie. You can't ask Eric Sevareid **how he knows** that the premise of his editorial is valid. You can't ask Bob Dylan **why** he switched from folk to rock to country music.

Conjecture about such matters is called "criticism." But the critics also appear in the mass media, and are therefore no more accessible than the sources. Teachers, however, can serve as accessible critics and should. But in the end, each man must be his own best critic, his qualifications for the job notwithstanding.

In our culture, the bulk of criticism concerns those two perennial topics—Sex and Violence (or Eros and Thantos, or Love and War, or Life and Death, etc., etc., etc.). It seems highly unlikely that these two topics will be—or can be—eliminated from mass entertainment, any more than they can be eliminated from art or life. No amount of censorship and ranting discourse will be able to erase concern with

"Teachers, preachers, parents, and legislators have asked us **(the social scientists)** a thousand times over these past fifteen years whether violence in the media produces delinquency, whether the escapist nature of much of the fare does not blind people to reality, and just what the media can do to the political persuasions of their audiences. To these questions we have not only failed to provide definite answers, but we have done something worse: we have provided evidence in partial support of every hue of every view."

—Joseph T. Klapper,
The Effects of Mass Communication

these themes, much to the consternation of a legion of critics, so we may as well resign ourselves to those facts, and resolve to deal with them honestly.

There are several views of the roles of mass media in presenting and portraying these themes. Briefly and simply stated, the views include:

1) The violence-begets-violence, sex-begets (period) point-of-view, wherein the "monkey see, monkey do" concept is maintained. All manner of mayhem and moral deviation is attributed to the moment that somebody saw something he shouldn't have and took it to heart.

2) The "immunity" theory, wherein we are led to believe that even if the media do not effect our actions directly, they do, at least, create a passive indifference to immorality and violence which carries over to our everyday lives, implying that most of us are incapable of distinguishing between fantasy and reality.

3) The "catharsis" theory, wherein we are told that vicarious violence and/or moral turpitude provide a handy, healthy substitute, which in turn eliminates the need for the real thing.

4) The "pessimistic" view, an in-between opinion, which tends toward the thesis that personal predisposition and a "nexus of mediating factors" affect the effects, and that, in general, media are probably more apt to reinforce existing attitudes and opinions

"Concern about the possible influence of mass communication upon the opinions and attitudes of men has been prevalent for several decades and has existed, in a less intense way, as long as there have been mass or quasi-mass communications. The figure of the pen as mightier than the sword has been modernized by social observers who have claimed that the mass media are more powerful than the atomic bomb. Other social observers have scoffed. As the more fearful have pointed to the impressive successes of various propaganda campaigns, the more phlegmatic have pointed to the impressive failures of other campaigns. Neither group has been hard put to find evidence to support its position."

—Klapper, **The Effects of Mass Communication**

than to create new ones.

And, THE ANSWER is (check one):

1) "monkey see, monkey do"
2) "immunity"
3) "catharsis"
4) "pessimism"
5) All of the above.
6) None of the above.
7) Who knows?

None of the four views has been proved beyond the shadow of a doubt to date; but as Paul Simon says, "A man hears what he wants to hear and disregards the rest."

Many have heard what they want to hear and **all** they want to hear. What they tend to disregard is the empirical socio-psychological research, which, on the whole, is inconclusive at best, and certainly not as simplistic as some of the Forçes for Good in the Community would have us believe.

Forces for Good in the Community, characters recurring throughout this book, are those people who have very definite, narrowly defined ideas about what is "good"—not only for themselves but for everyone else as well—and who attempt to force their subjective value judgments on the entire community. The Forces have often confused the entire issue of mass media effects by misusing limited existing evidence simply to shore up their personal opinions. I have little patience with their hypocrisy.

"Marshall McLuhan, who, as just about everybody ought to know by now, is the Canadian agricultural expert and author of 'The Romance of Wheat'—No! I am mistaken . . ."

—Michael J. Arlen

"He is the Wizard of Oz, and we are Dorothys from flat, clean Kansas . . ."

—Richard Goldstein

"Suppose he **is** what he sounds like, the most important thinker since Newton, Darwin, Freud, Einstein, and Pavlov—What if he is right?"

—Tom Wolfe

"If I have inadvertently suggested that **Understanding Media** is pure nonsense, let me correct that impression. It is impure nonsense, nonsense adulterated by sense."

—Dwight Macdonald

"Marshall McLuhan, whadaya doin'?"

—Henry Gibson

The effects of media on a mass scale will not be determined in the course of the Electric Humanities, but at least it affords us an opportunity to discuss effects on the personal level, and that's a start.

mcluhan

He is called the "Oracle of Pop," "The Guru of Mass Media." He is a Canadian professor of English literature, whose books and articles have brought him international notoriety as an iconoclastic philosopher of the electronic age. He is Herbert Marshall McLuhan.

Marshall McLuhan is neither empirical nor emotional. Futhermore, he is not concerned with the sex and violence quotients of media, but rather with the effects of media in terms of the changes they create in man and society by shaping perceptions and our images of ourselves.

McLuhan's ideas are flamboyant, cryptic, challenging, controversial, and important. They contain implications which may affect all of our social institutions, especially education.

Media, in McLuhanese (by his definition, including not only print, film, television, radio, but clothing, housing, money, automobiles, weapons, etc. as well), are all "extensions of some human faculty—psychic or physical."

"If these 'mass media' should serve only to weaken or corrupt previously achieved levels of verbal and pictorial culture, it won't be because there's anything inherently wrong with them. It will be because we've failed to master them as new languages in time to assimilate them to our total cultural heritage."

—McLuhan,
"Classroom Without Walls"

"NOBODY yet knows the language inherent in the new technological culture; we are all deaf-blind mutes in terms of the new situation. Our most impressive words and thoughts betray us by referring to the previously existent, not the present."

—McLuhan, "Five Sovereign Fingers Taxed The Breath" in **Explorations in Communication**

As we move from an era of print-dominated (linear) media into an era of electronic (non-linear) media, we are suffering, according to McLuhan, a social upheaval brought on by man's inability to make the appropriate transitions. We attempt to cling to the comfortable concepts of the past instead of adjusting ourselves to the demands of the present and the future.

Our old, fragmented vision of the world, says McLuhan, is no longer valid now that the media expand our perspective, involving us all with one another, and re-shaping the world in the image of a "global village."

As critic George P. Elliot says, "If he (McLuhan) is wrong, it matters."

While I am not suggesting that McLuhan be introduced in the classroom as the last word on media effects, I would certainly advocate his introduction as a featured speaker. His pop-art paperback, **The Medium Is The Massage,** contains all the basic McLuhanisms, enhanced by a collage of graphics by Quentin Fiore. Also available are a record album—the audio equivalent of **The Medium Is The Massage** (Columbia CS 9501) and a film version, produced by NBC's EXPERIMENT IN TELEVISION ("This Is Marshall McLuhan: The Medium Is The Massage"—distributed by Contemporary/McGraw-Hill).

"McLuhan didn't invent electricity or put kids in front of TV sets; he is merely trying to describe what's happening out there so that it can be dealt with intelligently. When someone warns you of an oncoming truck, it's frightfully impolite to accuse him of driving the thing."

—John Culkin, "A Schoolman's Guide to Marshall McLuhan" in **McLuhan: Pro & Con**

"I don't explain—
I explore."

—Marshall McLuhan

If only by creating "innumerable confusions," McLuhan is bound to stimulate discussion, debate, outright argument, and some desire for further exploration into the mysteries of the media. Motivating investigation is his avowed purpose, and a healthy concern about that which is confusing is a first step toward learning.

That his observations are drawn from popular as well as traditional culture has given some of his critics the ammunition to attack him as a "popularizer," but that which is "popular" is, by definition, "intended for people generally" and "liked by many people" and therefore, exactly what we need. Ideas are not to be dismissed simply because of their popularity.

Young people have been instrumental in the development of the McLuhan mystique, and, as John Culkin says, "McLuhan can help kids learn stuff better."

electric anthropology

The anthropological approach is applied to the study of folk cultures from that of the Trobriand Islander to that of the Alaskan Eskimo, but it is seldom applied in the study of our own society. In anthropology, the nature of a culture is deduced by examining its art and artifacts, its myth and ritual, its folkways and folklore. All of these elements exist, of course, within our own culture, but by virtue of ours being much more alive than dead, more familiar than foreign, and the fact that each of us is caught in the middle of it, we tend to neglect our option to step back and take a look at just what it is we're all caught up in.

"A man went looking for America. And couldn't find it anywhere . . ."

—ad for EASY RIDER

"The threat of nothingness is the danger of replacing American dreams by American illusions. Or replacing the ideals by the images . . ."

—Daniel J. Boorstin, **The Image or What Happened to the American Dream.**

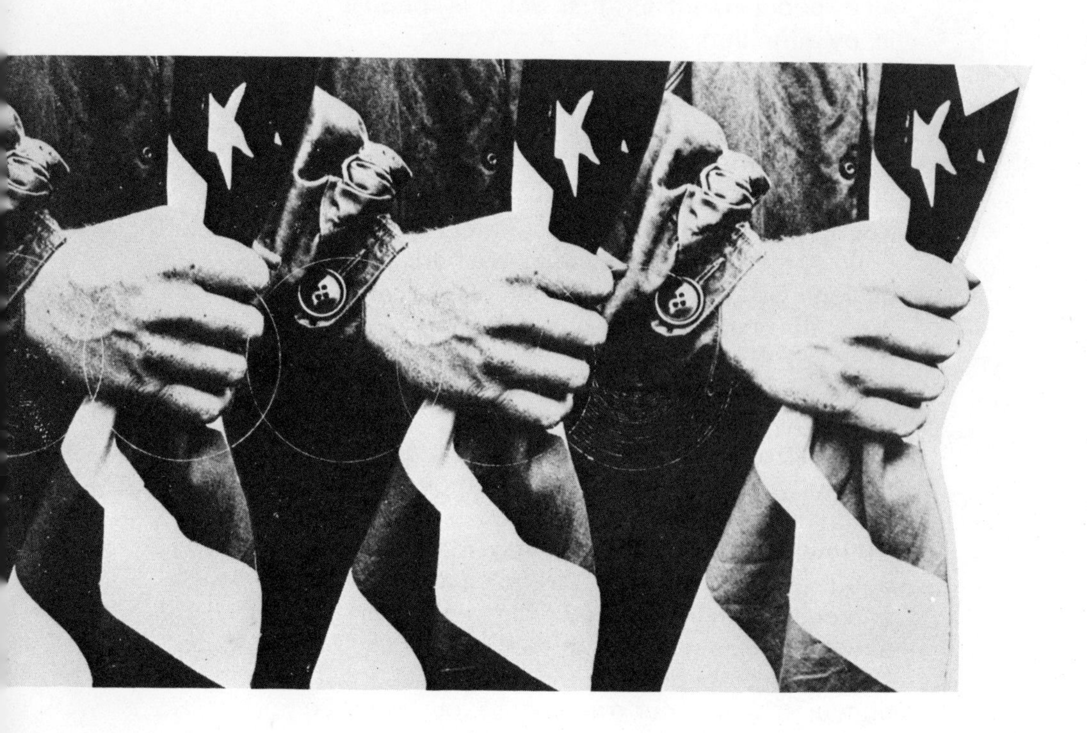

The term "culture," as it is used here, is to be spelled with the small c. The culture with which we will be dealing is not the "high culture" on display in our art museums, symphony halls, and repertory theatres, but rather the other culture as exhibited on billboards, jukeboxes, and silver screens, large and small. What this culture may lack in aesthetics, prestige, and respectability, it attempts to compensate for in mass appeal, mass availability, and mass consumption.

In speaking of "masses" (a recurrent term throughout the book), it is important to keep in mind that the masses are "us"—not "them."

There is always a Cultural Mafia around, determined to decry the popular. Teachers are often among the most susceptible converts to the kind of cultural blackmail that puts down the low- and middle-brow, insisting self-righteously that reading is somehow innately more virtuous than viewing, that Art is **always** infinitely preferable to entertainment, and that popular pleasures are insufferably imbecilic.

The "bad taste" of the "common man" is an unending source of dismay to the elitist, and a certain smug, snide, superior tone underlies his accusations. In America, the "common man" (us, again) is usually impervious to the criticism.

"Does trash corrupt? A nutty Puritanism still flourishes in the arts, not just in the school teachers' approach of wanting art to be 'worthwhile,' but in the higher reaches of the academic life with those idealogues who denounce us for enjoying trash as if this enjoyment took us away from the really disturbing, angry new art of our time and somehow destroyed us. If we had to **justify** our trivial silly pleasures, we'd have a hard time."

—Pauline Kael, "Trash, Art and Movies" in **Going Steady**

In school, he was told what he **should** like, and that what he **did** like was a worthless waste of time. He apparently didn't believe it, and now he "doesn't know much about art but he knows what he likes." And what he likes, for the most part, is masspop, all that incriminating education notwithstanding.

A basic misconception seems to be the prevailing notion that the two cultures exist as entirely separate entities. In fact, the popular culture is often only a simpler version of the high culture, and both are essentially manifestations of the human experience. As such, the themes of both cultures are invariably similar, and the major difference lies in the author/artist's ability to articulate his idea. The distinction might be compared to that between art and craftsmanship.

Sophistication demands sophistication. Simplicity makes no demands. But no one is born sophisticated, and we ask too much when we ask the young to change their cultural alliances in midstream, instead of encouraging a developmental and integral sophistication, allowing the uninitiated to appreciate that which is valuable throughout the entire spectrum of the cultural hierarchy, and to see similarities in all aspects of human expression. It need not be an either/or proposition.

"When the gods wish to punish us, they make us believe our own advertising."

—Daniel J. Boorstin (after Oscar Wilde), **The Image**

In our anthropological analysis of contemporary American culture, things are further complicated by the abundance of subcultures—regional, ethnic, and generational—which make modern American society a heterogeneous crazy quilt of life-styles, cross-pollinated by the mass media which show everybody everybody else, instigating instant fads and fashions in every area from attire to ideas.

The representative artifacts of our over-all popular culture are readily available for examination. They are our images and icons, our art and our ads—a pop-pourri of paraphernalia and memorabilia, some of it silly, some of it serious. Be it toys or technology, all of it can prove interesting, and these are the materials to be collected and considered in connection with the Electric Humanities.

adeas & The American Dream

"Plastic," in the current vernacular, is used to describe that which is phoney, false, without real substance, simulated reality. That which is plastic, be it person, place, or thing, is only an image of the real McCoy.

We are often warned that, in a society where plastic images take on immense importance, we run the risk of losing track of our realities altogether.

The use of images is immediately associated with the field of advertising, and by extension, all media must be considered advertisement of.

"The use of mass psychoanalysis to guide campaigns of persuasion has become the basis of a multimillion-dollar industry. Professional persuaders have seized upon it in their groping for more effective ways to sell us their wares—whether products, ideas, attitudes, candidates, goals, or states of mind."

—Vance Packard, **The Hidden Persuaders**

"The image of America overshadows the ideals of America."

—Daniel J. Boorstin, **The Image**

a sort, not for commercial products alone, but for myths, attitudes, life-styles, ideas, and the most coveted, most elusive mirage of them all—the American Dream.

As an illustrative exercise in ad imagery, compile an American Dream collage from those images perpetrated in magazine advertisements, on TV commercials, on billboards, etc. See how close it comes to what you think life is all about.

A cardinal rule in the study of communication is that the symbol is **not to be confused with** that which it symbolizes. The same rule applies to the ad image. Their respective images notwithstanding, obviously cigarettes are not to be equated with manliness, automobiles are not automatic sex appeal, under-arm deodorants are not the key to friendship and social acceptance, etc.

On the conscious level, all of us would probably deny susceptibility to the shallow images of such ads, but the appeals seem to be made not to the conscious but to the subconscious, where they reinforce the old ingrained myths, relegated by maturity to the back of the mind.

When the "hype" (image manipulation) is applied to selling soap, it doesn't seem all that serious. When it is applied to peddling presidential candidates, it should be of considerable conern to us all.

"Big Government and Big Business already possess, or will very soon possess, all the techniques for mind-manipulation described in **Brave New World,** along with others of which I was too unimaginative to dream."

—Aldous Huxley, **Brave New World Revisited**

"Propaganda ceases where simple dialogue begins."

—Jacques Ellul, **Propaganda**

We have all read the frightening and foreboding speculations of society manipulated by mass communications as fictionalized by Huxley, Orwell, and others, but hopefully such nightmares are avoidable as long as individual awareness prevails. An ongoing analysis of WHAT we are being told, HOW it is being told to us, WHO is telling it and WHY would seem to be the best preventive measure to be taken against the image manipulators.

Familiarity with the "hidden persuaders" has, it seems, bred some degree of contempt for them among the young today. The search for superficial "status symbols" is a mode of living which has been seriously questioned by many young people, and rightfully so. That our principal preoccupation in an era of enormous social upheaval should be conspicuous consumption is patently absurd. That newsphotos of dying soldiers in Indochina, starving children in Africa, or riots in our city streets should be directly juxtaposed with inane ads for dishwashing detergents or mouthwash is a grievous insult to our intelligence and humanity.

If, in the Electric Humanities, we can develop an acute awareness among our kids of advertising techniques, and also encourage a healthy skepticism about image manipulation, we will, I believe, be rendering a valuable and important educational and social service.

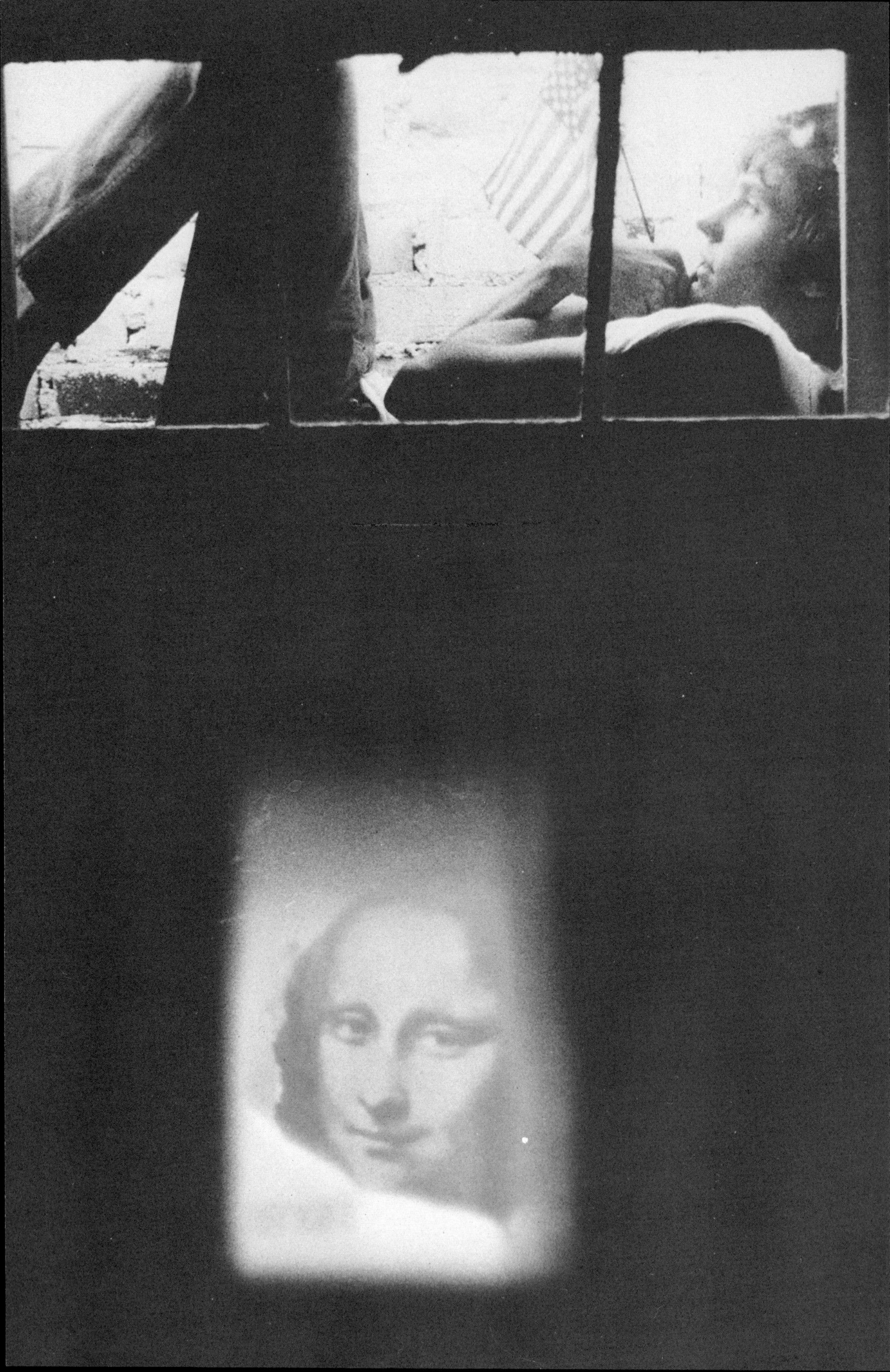

From the general view of the Electric Environment as outlined here, we now move on to some of the nitty-gritty, the specific sources of our popular culture and contemporary mythology.

Although, for purposes of organization, the several media are treated separately, we should keep in mind that they are all actually interrelated. McLuhan contends that the content of one medium is another medium—see the hit movie, based on the Broadway play, based on the best-selling novel, based on the popular song, based on the passing remark, etc.

What is not lost in the translation from one medium to another is the basic mythos, common to all media entertainment and to our way of life.

THE ELECTRIC ENVIRONMENT:
an incomplete bibliography

communications, personal

Don Fabun,
Communications: The Transfer of Meaning (Kaiser Aluminum News/ Glencoe Press, Macmillan Co.)

communications, mass

Joseph T. Klapper,
The Effects of Mass Communication (Free Press)

William L. Rivers & Wilbur Schramm, **Responsibility in Mass Communication** (Harper & Row)

Harold Mendelsohn,
Mass Entertainment (College & University Press)

Jacques Ellul,
Propaganda: The Formation of Men's Attitudes (Alfred A. Knopf)

mcluhan

Marshall McLuhan,
Understanding Media (McGraw-Hill/Signet)
The Gutenberg Galaxy (University of Toronto Press/Signet)
The Mechanical Bride (Vanguard Press)
Culture Is Our Business (McGraw-Hill)

with Quentin Fiore:
The Medium is the Massage (Bantam)
War & Peace in the Global Village (Bantam)

with Edmund Carpenter (editors):
Explorations in Communication (Beacon)

Gerald Emanuel Stearn (ed.),
McLuhan: Hot and Cool (Signet)

Raymond Rosenthal (ed.),
McLuhan: Pro and Con (Pelican)

electric anthropology

Tom Wolfe,
The Kandy-Kolored Tangerine-Flake Streamline Baby (Farrar, Straus, Giroux/Pocket Books)
The Pump House Gang (Farrar, Straus, Giroux/Bantam)
The Electric Kool-Aid Acid Test (Farrar, Straus, Giroux/Bantam)

Joan Didion,
Slouching Towards Bethlehem
(Macmillan Co./Delta)

on images & ads

Daniel J. Boorstin,
The Image or What Happened To The American Dream
(Atheneum)

Aldous Huxley,
Brave New World Revisited
(Harper & Row)

Vance Packard,
The Hidden Persuaders
(David McKay Co./Pocket Books)

general reference

Theodore Roszak,
The Making of a Counter Culture
(Doubleday/Anchor)

David Riesman,
Nathan Glazer, Reuel Denney,
The Lonely Crowd (Yale University Press/Anchor)

Susan Sontag,
Against Interpretation
(Farrar, Straus, Giroux/Dell)

Alvin Toffler,
Future Shock (Random House)

FU MANCHU

BEST
ORIGINAL

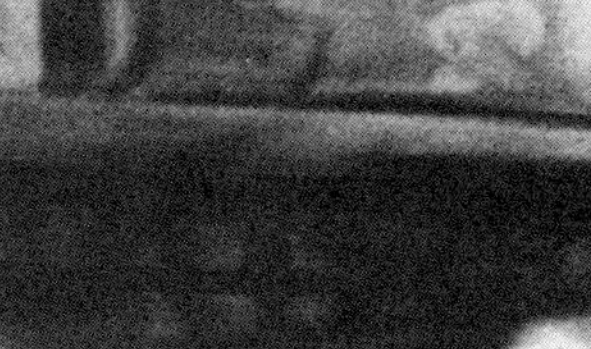

COLLECTORS
ALBUM
"SUPER HEROES WITH SUPER PROBLEMS"
Fantastic Four
He's COOL!! Wildest of the new, groovy...
THE INCREDIBLE
HULK
THE MIGHTY
THOR!
TARZAN
of the Apes
Edgar Rice Burroughs
THE SPIDER MASTER OF MEN!
THE SPIDER STRIKES!
THE MAN OF BRONZE

SCIENCE FICTION

". . . the comic book was feared and scorned and rejected from the classroom. Its good and bad features in form and content, when carefully set beside other kinds of art and narrative, could have become a major asset to the teacher."

—Marshall McLuhan,
"Classroom Without Walls"

THE DRUGSTORE LIBRARY

The place is called The Book Fair. It is a dingy despository of popular print, dealing in old magazines and dog-eared paperbacks.

The "stacks" of The Book Fair are simply organized (no Dewey decimal system here)—Westerns, War, Science Fiction, Romance, etc. You can buy a World War II issue of **Life,** a paperback Plato, almost anything by Ian Fleming among this newsstand residue.

the comic book underground

On Tuesday and Thursday evenings and on Saturday afternoons, a cellar door is opened up and the A-1 Comic Collectors' Exchange is open for business.

The proprietor is a middle-aged commercial artist, and father of eight. His name is Jim Payne and he is an expert on the exotic esoterica of American pop art, commonly known as comic books.

Many of us collected comics when we were kids. Payne never quit. He once took out a bank loan for more than $1,000 to buy a friend's collection, which is a far cry from swapping two Walt Disneys for a Superman. He must be serious.

Payne has a personal collection of about two hundred comics and a commercial collection ("Buy-Sell-Trade") of thousands.

"Clark decided he must turn his titanic strength into channels that would benefit mankind . . . And so was created SUPERMAN, champion of the oppressed, the physical marvel who had sworn to devote his existence to helping those in need."

—Jerome Siegel &
Joe Schuster, The Origin of
SUPERMAN

"Criminals are a superstitious cowardly lot, so my disguise must be able to strike terror into their hearts. I must be a creature of the night, black, terrible . . . a . . . a . . .
(As if in answer, a huge bat flies in the open window) . . . A bat! That's it! It's an omen . . .
I shall become a BAT!"

—Bruce Wayne's soliloquy in
THE LEGEND OF THE
BATMAN—WHO HE IS AND
HOW HE CAME TO BE
by Bob Kane

The rare ones, protected by plastic bags, go for two dollars or more (original price: 10¢). The library is carefully catalogued according to titles or genre.

Payne subscribes to **The Rocket Blast Comic Collector, The New York Review of Books** for comic book buffs. In the comic book underground, there are also hundreds of "fanzines"—newsletters featuring comic book commentary, in-depth analysis of particular characters, current price lists, reproductions and amateur art. The fanzines are circulated throughout the country.

Not long ago, Payne attended the Multi-Con in Oklahoma City, one of many regional conventions for collectors of comics, old radio programs, movie serials, and other pop culture artifacts. The admission fee was $3.50 plus an additional $5.00 for a table on which he set up shop, displaying his wares. He bought $300 worth of comics, sold a few, met a lot of nice people, and had a real swell time. The guest speaker was Buster Crabbe.

At the exchange, Payne is usually surrounded by a small (in numbers and size) retinue of kids, debating the comparative virtues of the Silver Surfer, Sub-Mariner or a host of other superhumans. Payne is their guru. He claims a devoted clientele of nostalgic adults as well as the kids. When the kids discover him, however, they are hesitant to spread the word for fear of encouraging encroachers who might ransack

"MAD brought into the malt shops the same angry abuse of middle-class America which comics like Mort Sahl and Lenny Bruce were to begin brirging into the night clubs of the mid-fifties. The kids who were twelve when MAD first appeared are in their early twenties now—and they have had a decade's experience in treating the stuff of their parents' lives as contemptible laughing stock."

—Roszak, **The Making of a Counter Culture**

"Hoo Hah!"

—MAD

the treasure trove known only to the select few. Their guarded knowledge, of course, presents an economic hassle for Payne who is stuck with many more comics than his handful of young followers are likely to buy. But he is the first to admit that it's a crazy business anyway, and he seems resigned to it as a labor of love.

We talked about our favorite artists—Frank Frazetta, Wally Wood, Jack Davis, Joe Kubert, Will Eisner, Al Williamson, and others. We reminisced about the golden age—the pre-comics code era when the fantasy masters made their masterpieces. Thumbing through his collection, I was transported twenty years back into a time when dreams cost a dime, and 20¢ of my quarter-a-week allowance invariably went for comics.

In junior high on Thursday afternoons, a gang of us would assault the corner drugstore, ravaging their piles of comics in search of new issues of TWO-FISTED TALES or INCREDIBLE SCIENCE FICTION or that 10¢ worth of pure insanity called MAD ("Humor in a Jugular Vein"). But a few titles like TALES FROM THE CRYPT and VAULT OF HORROR eventually put an end to that epoch.

Dr. Frederic Wertham, a New York psychiatrist and a Force for Good in the Community if ever there was one, insisted, with our parents' consent and approval, on protecting our minds whether we wanted them protected or not.

"Comic books, first of all, are junk. To accuse them of being what they are is to make no accusation at all: there is no such thing as **uncorrupt** junk or **moral** junk or **educational** junk—though attempts at the latter have, from time to time, been foisted on us. But education is not the purpose of junk . . . Junk is there to entertain on the basest most compromised of levels . . . Junk is a second-class citizen of the arts; a status of which we and it are constantly aware. There are certain inherent privileges in second-class citizenship. Irresponsibility is one. Not being taken seriously is another. Junk, like the drunk at the wedding, can get away with doing or saying anything because, by its very appearance, it is already in disgrace. It has no one's respect to lose; no image to endanger. Its values are the least middle class of all the mass media. That's why it is needed so."

—Jules Feiffer,
The Great Comic Book Heroes

The Doctor and the Forces embarked on a crusade against the comics (a feat which Wertham recently repeated when he led the attack on TV cartoons for kids). With the subsequent installation of the Comics Code Authority, we found ourselves confined to the "good clean fun" of Mickey Mouse and Donald Duck (which wasn't much fun at all) or the cultural enrichment of CLASSICS ILLUSTRATED (good for faking your book reports, but worthless as entertainment). Naturally, the comic book business took a dive.

Though I suppose I'd have to agree that some of the '50s comics were grotesque, I've also learned that much of Wertham's "empirical evidence" concerning the comics is scientifically dubious. I can only speak for myself as an average avid comic fan. The comics got me hooked on reading. In their way, they turned me on to art. They stimulated my imagination, but I never committed an ax murder, or even considered it.

After almost a decade, a semi-renaissance came about in the comic book business when Marvel Comics resurrected many of the super-heroes of yore. The Marvel mags were sufficiently sophisticated to seduce again the kids who had been caught by the Comics Code. Those kids were in college now, and could often be seen carrying a copy of THE FANTASTIC FOUR with their textbooks for Eighteenth Century Poetry & Prose. Among

"Many are the superheroes who have risen from the carnage and the devastation of World War II . . . but none more gallant, none more daring, none more inspiring than the red-white-and-blue clad avenger who has fired the imagination of freedom-loving fans.

"Where is the heart that does not beat faster at the mere mention of his glory-studded name? Where is the pulse that does not quicken at the sight of his lithe, muscular form—his flashing shield—his colorful costume? Where is the spy, the traitor, the murderous arch-fiend who does not tremble in unabashed terror at the awesome sight of democracy's greatest defender?

". . . the most universally honored hero of his time—the dazzling human dynamo whom men call . . . CAPTAIN AMERICA."

—Stan Lee, Introduction to **Captain America: The Great Gold Steal** their younger brothers and sisters, a new audience was on its way again.

It is a long way from Billy Batson shazamming himself into Captain Marvel to the anti-heroics of The Incredible Hulk, but all the basic appeals endure. Somehow, the world seems so much simpler when it can be segregated into star-spangled super-heroes and snarling super-villains.

paperback writer

Upstairs at The Book Fair, you find the comic books for grown-ups—words without pictures called paperback thrillers. Despite the change in format, the basic mythology stays the same.

The heritage of the paperbacks can be traced back to the earlier pulp magazines, the dime novels, and beyond. Over the years, a stock company of heroes—the hard-boiled detective, the guts-and-glory soldier, the legendary American cowboy, etc.—have emerged as the stereotypes of American popular fiction. New characters are seldom more than slight variations on the established themes, molded in the images of old archetypes, but in some cases, we find examples of writers who excel in a popular genre. Their kitsch is endowed with a craftsmanship which sets them apart from the company of hacks. The basic material may be much the same—but the unique talent of a Zane Grey, and Edgar Rice Burroughs, or a Dashiell Hammett can make a kind of magic of it.

"As the great muscles of the man's back and
shoulders knotted beneath the tension of his
efforts, and the huge biceps and forearm
held at bay those mighty tusks, the veil of
centuries of civilization and culture was
swept from the blurred vision of the
Baltimore girl.

"When the long knife drank deep a dozen
times of Terkoz' heart's blood, and the
great carcass rolled lifeless upon the ground,
it was a primeval woman who sprang forward
with outstretched arms toward the primeval man
who had fought for her and won her.

"And Tarzan?
He did what no red-blooded man needs lessons
in doing. He took the woman in his arms and
smothered her upturned, panting lips with kisses.

"For a moment, Jane lay there with half-closed
eyes. For a moment—the first in her young life—
she knew the meaning of love."

—Edgar Rice Burroughs,
Tarzan of the Apes

The best of these authors from the Drugstore Library often endure long after the more "serious" novelists of their day have faded into oblivion. The pop creations are revived again and again to be enjoyed by several generations, and to serve as the modern equivalent of folk-tales. The best of these authors are master storytellers whose originality and imagination seem to make them immune to time and changes, yet they are seldom, if ever, taken seriously in terms of "literature;" their work is disregarded as "escapist" fare.

There is nothing inherently wrong with escapism. A constant concentration on the personal and social problems that beset a man today would be enough to make any of us crazy. "Escapism" offers a reprieve, a much-needed release from the tensions of the times. Escapist literature does not have to be taken seriously. That's the strongest point in its favor.

contemporary mythology

How seriously have we taken the mythology common to popular literature and the other pop media? If repetition alone can have any subliminal effect, the myths may be deeply ingrained indeed.

Sentimentalism, violence, and Puritanism (or our latter-day reverse-Puritanism) are easily recognizable as trademarks of pop literature, and as predominant characteristics of our myths. The recognition and

"Tonight, we begin carrying out the ideals of my father—to go here and there, from one end of the world to the other, looking for excitement and adventure, striving to help those who need help, and punishing those who deserve it."

—Doc Savage addresses his troops in **Doc Savage: Man of Bronze** by Kenneth Robeson

"(Conan's) gods were simple and understandable; Crom was their chief, and he lived on a great mountain, whence he sent forth dooms and death. It was useless to call on Crom, because he was a gloomy, savage god, and he hated weaklings. But he gave a man courage at birth, and the will and might to kill his enemies, which in the Cimmerian's mind, was all any god should be expected to do."

—Robert E. Howard, "The Tower of The Elephant" in **Conan**

discussion of modern American mythology is a major reason for the inclusion of the Drugstore Library in the Electric Humanities. As we shall see, these are intermedia myths, but most of them originated in our popular literature.

For example:

The "Good Guys & Bad Guys" Myth: The world seems simpler when divided into heroes and villains. Such simplification, however, when applied to our everyday lives, results in the creation of US vs. THEM dichotomies. WE, of course, are always the Good Guys; THEY are the baddies. WE wear the white hats; THEY wear the black. All reason, experience, and observation indicate the falsity of such categorical notions. Shades of gray, we know, prevail over black and white, and yet we seem to find ourselves suckered into accepting the US vs. THEM proposition time and time again. Of all the myths to be found in our popular culture, this one is surely the most dominant and the most dangerous. A society plagued by political, racial, and generational conflicts, and a world armed to the teeth with overkill potential, can scarcely afford melodramatic showdowns between US and THEM.

The "Might Makes Right" Myth: The pop hero, as a rule, is portrayed as a being blessed with both better brains and better brawn. Of the two attributes, the latter inevitably proves more useful than the former. Physical

"I happen to be on my way to New York, Blunton, to meet one of the greatest criminals of all times, a man whose nature is so cunning and, at the same time so brutal, that it is a delight to fight him. Compared to him, you are a repulsive child, a contemptible card-sharp, who affords me some trifling excitement to break the monotony of this trip."

—Richard Wentworth
("The Spider") to a minor foe
in **The Spider Strikes** by
R.T.M. Scott
(Grant Stockbridge)

aggression, of course, makes for more exciting episodes than does logical discourse, but the underlying idea seems to be that the strong are somehow entitled to the privilege of imposing their will on the weak, who by virtue of their weakness relinquish certain rights. This kind of Ayn Randishness takes us back to the law of the jungle, and seems less than viable in a contemporary social context.

The "His Strength Is The Strength Of Ten Because His Heart Is Pure" Myth: Our hero is not only physically and mentally on top, but he is morally superior as well. There is always the unspoken implication that God (or, at least, the best interests of Truth and Justice) is on his side, thereby legitimizing all his undertakings. Our hero is traditionally immune to self-doubt. A Hamlet makes a hopeless super-hero.

The "Up the Underdog" Myth: Everybody loves a loser as long as he eventually wins. It is never enough for our hero to triumph in a fair fight. Instead, he is called upon to overcome seemingly insurmountable odds to achieve a success which often apparently puts him in the position previously held by his oppressor—all of which may reflect our concern with competition, upward mobility, and status seeking. Pity the poor underdog who stays under, for he is a dog indeed.

"'I have heard of you, Doktor Zwantag, and perhaps you have heard of me. Have you ever heard of G-8 the American spy?'

'G-8!' repeated Zwantag. 'Ach, surely you do not means the master spy of the war? The famous young American who has received more curses from Germany and the great Intelligence system than any other living man?'

G-8 laughed.

'Right,' he said. 'You are looking at G-8 now in the guise of an Oberleutnant in the Kaiser's Imperial air force . . .'"

—Robert J. Hogan, **G-8 and His Battle Aces: Purple Aces**

The "Superiority Complex" Myth: Eligibility for heroism has, for the most part, required that candidates be white, Anglo-Saxon, males. For years, all others were condemned to the status of "trusty sidekicks" at best. In the wake of the civil rights movement, a few black pop heroes have begun to emerge (e.g. Marvel Comics' "Falcon"—sort of a Sidney Poitier in supergarb). And, if ever the ladies of the women's liberation crusade had legitimate cause for complaint, it would be the treatment of women in pop fiction, Wonder Woman notwithstanding.

The "Take The Law Into His Own Capable Hands" Myth: In popular novels, established channels of law enforcement always seem to be utterly ineffectual, and so our self-righteous hero must emerge as self-proclaimed vigilante and avenger of otherwise unpunished wrongs. Bob Dylan's line—"To live outside the law you must be honest"—exemplifies our hero. Here we have the influence of rugged individualism, an untimely but unchallenged American ideal. In the context of our 20th century social structure, such frontier ethics are of dubious value. One cannot help but wonder whether Lee Harvey Oswald, Jack Ruby, Sirhan Sirhan, and James Earl Ray might have seen themselves in some such "outlaw avenger" role.

The "Sex and The Single Super-Hero" Myth; A California school district once banned the Tarzan books from their libraries for lack of evidence that Tarzan and Jane were legally wed. There seemed to be the awful

myth n.

1. a traditional story serving to explain some phenomenon, custom, etc. 2. mythology. 3. any fictitious story, person, or thing.

—Webster

possibility that they were living in that tree in sin. That case must surely be one of the few indictments against an old-time pop hero for sexual/moral turpitude. Until recently, most of our heroes have been inclined to prove their manhood in fist fights instead of in the bedroom. Rescue without reward and a ride off alone into the sunset was, and often remains, the rule. (Could it be that their acts of aggression somehow provided a sexual substitute? Shades of Norman Mailer . . .) At any rate, unrequited love was usually the order of the day, whereas today, love (or even mild attraction) is usually anything but unrequited. In pop literature, there seem to be two basic ways of dealing with sex: ignoring it or overdoing it.

These are only a few of the myths to be found in popular literature. Further investigation will uncover many more. If the examples appear to be essentially negative, I would like to correct that impression in part with a reminder that the purpose of pop lit. is not to give moral instruction but simply to entertain. Most of us learn early on, I think, to make the appropriate distinctions between fantasy and reality, and we turn to pop for amusement rather than meaningful comment. Pop literature is not to be taken seriously, but in the spirit of fun and diversion. That, of course, is the main point to be put across to kids, in case they don't know it already.

". . . but he is no ordinary criminal. He is the greatest genius which the powers of evil have put on earth for centuries."

—Inspector Nayland Smith describes his arch-nemesis in **The Insidious Dr. Fu Manchu** by Sax Rohmer

On the positive side, pop lit. upholds many old-fashioned but not necessarily outworn virtues which may often be too easily forgotten in this age of the anti-hero. Take what you can use and leave the rest behind.

In recent years, the concept of "Camp" has taught us how to laugh at that which is hokey in our popular arts without denying ourselves the pleasures they still provide. I recommend the application of that principle to the study of the Drugstore Library as well as ensuing phases of the Electric Humanities.

a note on pop therapy

Like all English teachers, I have encountered numerous kids totally turned off by reading, perhaps because the visual culture which surrounds them offers many easier alternatives.

We find that the kid who can't hack **Silas Marner** may still respond to something like **Doc Savage.** To insist that **Silas Marner** is preferable is a sure-fire way to make him give up on reading altogether. The smart move, of course, is to encourage an interest in reading, whatever the material may be. Most kids will eventually want more.

Although remedial reading has not been a function of the Electric Humanities, I do believe that pop literature offers excellent opportunities in that area. Such an approach

". . . a long, reverberating sound came to the
ears of the astonished men. It was a laugh,
a vivid, creepy laugh; a laugh that was
real, and yet unnatural.

"It was the laugh of The Shadow!"

—Maxwell Grant, **The Living Shadow**

has already been outlined by Dr. Daniel N. Fader and Dr. Elton B. McNeil in their **Hooked On Books** program (Berkley Medallion Books), highly recommended for those interested.

THE DRUGSTORE LIBRARY:
an incompleat
annotated
bibliography

In terms of the Electric Humanities, popular literature is used mainly to reveal the roots of our popular culture. Many of the current pop lit. paperbacks are revivals of the pulp fiction from the pre-TV '30s and before, and nearly all of our present masspop entertainment is easily traced to these earlier forms.

Pop literature reflects, if not what we are, at least what we seem to think we might like to be. It's funky and it's fun. And the book reports are beautiful.

A limited bibliography for the Drugstore Library includes the following authors, titles, and genres—a representative cross-section, selected on the basis of proven popular appeal rather than any literary criteria. The list should be heavily supplemented by your own additions and those of your students.

—Edgar Rice Burroughs is the acknowledged master of the adventure-fantasy **oeuvre.** Burroughs' TARZAN has become an intermedia hero of the highest echelon. Another

"I am of another world, the great planet Earth, which revolves about our common sun and next within the orbit of your Barsoom, which we know as Mars. How I came here I cannot tell you for I do not know: but here I am . . ."

—John Carter explains himself to Princess Dejah Thoris in **A Princess of Mars** by Edgar Rice Burroughs

Burroughs hero, JOHN CARTER OF MARS, ranks with Buck Rogers and Flash Gordon as a star of science-fiction/fantasy. (Ballantine Books/Ace Books).

—Robert E. Howard's chronicles of CONAN THE BARBARIAN, hero of the Hyborian Age, (Lancer Books) are considered classics of the "Sword & Sorcery" school of pop lit., which has recently enjoyed a widespread revival due largely to the enormous success of J.R.R. Tolkien's LORD OF THE RINGS trilogy.

—Kenneth Robeson's DOC SAVAGE stories (Bantam), one of the many 1930s adventure series recently revived for the paperback market, pit the mind and muscle of the "Man of Bronze" and his crew of extraordinary colleagues against all manner of imaginative villainy.

—Maxwell Grant's THE SHADOW (Bantam/ Belmont) "knows what evil lurks in the hearts of men" and uses his supernatural talents to undo evil-doers in this series of detective thrillers.

—R.T.M. Scott's THE SPIDER—"Master of Men" is the sophisticated sleuth with a secret identity—a super-stereotype of the crime fighter category (Berkley).

—Robert J. Hogan's G-8 AND HIS BATTLE ACES (Berkley) features the aerodynamic exploits of "America's Flying Spy" and his two trusty sidekicks as they win World War I in their

"As a secret agent who held the rare double-O prefix—the license to kill in the Secret Service—it was his duty to be as cool about death as a surgeon. If it happened, it happened. Regret was unprofessional—worse, it was death-watch beetle in the soul."

—James Bond reflects on his career in **Goldfinger** by Ian Fleming

Hisso-powered Spads—shades of Snoopy, his Sopwith Camel, and the rotten Red Baron.

—Sax Rohmer's INSIDIOUS DR. FU MANCHU (Pyramid) is the super-villain, a bad guy for all seasons, whose sinister schemes are thwarted again and again by his arch-enemy, intrepid Englishman Nayland Smith.

—Ian Fleming's JAMES BOND books (Signet) gave us the British super-spy who most recently captured the public's imagination as he artfully disposed of a variety of villains, bent on world domination as is their wont.

—Stan Lee's MARVEL COMICS feature the derring-do of a sensational stable of superpeople like Captain America, The Mighty Thor, The Amazing Spider-Man, The Incredible Hulk, The Fantastic Four, The Sub-Mariner, The Silver Surfer, Dr. Strange, and others who offer some interesting new twists on the comic traditions.

—SUPERMAN D.C. COMICS (National Periodical Publications) star those ever-popular prototypes of pop—SUPERMAN and BATMAN—as well as a caped crowd of additional adventurers.

—MAD magazine and/or the MAD paperback books (Ballantine/Signet) focus their satirical attacks mainly on the mass media and popular culture, which makes MAD ideal for our purposes.

"That was the paralyzing challenge. The rustler turned a ghastly white. The frontier's bloody creed, by which he had lived, called him to his death. His green eyes set balefully. He knew. He showed his training. He had no more fear of death than of the swallows flitting under the eaves above. But he had a magnificent and desperate courage to take his enemy with him.

"Richardson never uttered a word. Almost imperceptibly his body lowered as if under instinct to crouch. His stiff bent right arm began to quiver.

"Nevada saw the thought in Richardson's eyes—the birth of the message to nerve and muscle. When his hand flashed down, Nevada was drawing . . ."

—the showdown from **Nevada**
by Zane Grey

The Ballantine paperbacks feature reprints of the original MAD comics with the weird wit of Harvey Kurtzman and the outstanding cartooning talents of Jack Davis, Wally Wood, and Bill Elder.

—Zane Grey is probably the papa of the pop Western—the central source of American mythology. The work of Grey (**Nevada, Riders of the Purple Sage,** and twenty-three more) as well as the work of western writers like Luke Short, Max Brand, Louis L'Amour, and Will Henry comes from a heritage which can be traced back to Jack London, Bret Harte, Mark Twain, and James Fenimore Cooper.

—Science Fiction is probably the most misunderstood area of popular literature. Some very serious writing by contemporary authors like Arthur C. Clarke, Robert Heinlein, Ray Bradbury, Isaac Asimov, and Kurt Vonnegut, Jr., has too often gone unnoticed because of the "escapist entertainment" treatment that science fiction has been accorded. In most pop literature, save the western, science plays an important but ambivalent role. Science is often the source and/or resource of the super-hero as well as a wicked weapon "in the wrong hands." If ever we had an accurate parallel between life and pop art, this would probably be it. As technology creates problems ranging from nuclear threat to ecological imbalance, we find ourselves turning to technology for the solutions. Our post-Prometheus super-heroes continue

"The popular audience has always demanded the pseudo-fiction of terror, which in all of its major forms Poe perfected for the American market-place: the ghost story, the detective story, and science fiction."

—Leslie A. Fiedler, **Love and Death in the American Novel** to wage scientific warfare with an endless array of "mad scientists" (Frankenstein Lives!). For those who aren't freaked out by future shock, the study of science fiction, from Jules Verne and H.G. Wells to Aldous Huxley and George Orwell, can offer a number of interesting speculations as to where we are and where we might be going.

—Horror has its charms. As anyone who has taught American literature knows, Edgar Allan Poe will always turn 'em on. There are elements of the horror story in nearly every pop lit. genre (again excluding the Western, although I once saw an ad for a movie entitled BILLY THE KID MEETS DRACULA—the ultimate synthesis of pop forms). Poe's tales of terror, H.P. Lovecraft's creepy classics, the Gothic novels, those Alfred Hitchcock anthologies of the eerie—all attest to our fascination with the bizarre and the macabre, the unexplained, our dark interests in the idea of death.

—Romance is the catchword of pop fiction for girls, a field with which I am admittedly unfamiliar. The major writers, if only in terms of their prolific outputs, seem to be Emilie Loring, Kathleen Norris, and Grace Livingston Hill. A casual perusal of a few of these books leads me to suspect that they portray the feminine version of the American Dream in terms of a brief, colorful career (e.g., as nurses, fashion models, actresses, etc.), culminating in love and marriage.

"Certain elements of the underground faith of the eighteenth century have come to seem to us absurd; but we live still in the Age of the Novel (and of the cinema which is its child), so that no matter how vulgarized the sentimental myth may have become, no matter how smugly we snicker at it, we are somehow still its victims and beneficiaries."

—Fiedler, **Love and Death in the American Novel**

Please seek further information on romantic pop lit. from knowledgeable sources like teenage girl students.

This brief bibliography leaves a great deal to further exploration. There is much that has gone unmentioned; wander through any large paperback bookstore to see just how much there is. A complete consideration of any one of the areas touched upon here would easily require an entire volume. I can only suggest that student interest will help to develop a larger listing, and will open up additional investigations of popular literature not considered here. Along with comic books and paperbacks, material like newspaper comic strips and popular magazines also warrant attention. Develop your own special approach to the Drugstore Library, based on the reading of your kids.

Most importantly, make it enjoyable in respect for the authors' original intentions.

additional references

Jules Feiffer,
The Great Comic Book Heroes (Dial Press)

George Perry & Alan Aldridge,
The Penguin Book of Comics (Penguin Books)

Pierre Couperie & Maurice C. Horn,
A History of The Comic Strip
(Crown Publishers)

Dick Lupoff & Don Thompson, editors,
All In Color For A Dime (Arlington House)

Tony Goodstone,
The Pulps (Chelsea House)

"With his faithful Indian companion, Tonto,
the daring and resourceful Masked Rider of
the Plains led the fight for law and order
in the early western United States. Nowhere
in the pages of history can one find a greater
champion of justice! Return with us now to those
thrilling days of yesteryear! From out of the past,
come the thundering hoofbeats of the great
horse, Silver! The Lone Ranger rides again!"

—announcer Fred Foy
introduces THE LONE
RANGER radio show

in the oral tradition: folk tales

In primitive societies, the myths and legends are passed from generation to generation through the folk tales recited at tribal gatherings.

Our own society once had a similar oral tradition. It was called radio.

It was not radio as we know it now (to be explored in a later chapter), but rather a large polished wooden cabinet, filled with glowing tubes, fun, and fables.

The radio of yore provides an apropos postscript to the Drugstore Library, because the "golden age" of radio closely paralleled the "golden age" of pop pulp and comics; these media were thoroughly integrated. Tarzan, Superman, Batman, and The Lone Ranger were among the panoply of intermedia heroes who went on into movies and television, thereby establishing themselves in the pantheon of pop.

I can still recall my own disappointment as a kid when I chanced upon a magazine photo of a radio studio in which one of my favorite programs was in production. The studio was merely a tableau of broadcasting equipment and very ordinary looking people—one of my earliest disillusionments. Until that time, I believed that the adventures of Sergeant Preston and King, for instance, were being transmitted to me direct from the Yukon—"on location."

". . . We had a Philco radio. It was about six feet tall, had 287 knobs on it, of which only two worked: OFF-ON-VOLUME and STATION SELECTOR."

—Bill Cosby, "Chicken Heart"

A crushing revelation, and one that points up old radio's most appealing quality. Like the novel, but unlike film and TV, it required extensive use of the imagination.

Comedian Bill Cosby captures the kind of involvement generated by early radio in his memorable "Chicken Heart" routine. Recounting another of his episodes from childhood, Cosby describes sneaking out of bed after his parents have gone out for the evening to listen to LIGHTS OUT! (Arch Oboler's popular suspense-horror show of the '30s and '40s, which did, in fact, once feature the program described by Cosby).

On LIGHTS OUT!, the little kid Cosby hears the tale of "The Chicken Heart That Ate Up New York City." After eating up the Empire State Building and the Jersey Turnpike, the monster chicken heart is reported to be on its way to "your home town!" It is at this point that Cosby invented his famous formula for keeping monsters away—smear Jello all over the floor and set the sofa on fire. He is rescued from the impending chicken heart when his father comes home and turns off the radio. This hilarious little folk tale about folk tales can be heard on Bill Cosby's WONDERFULNESS album (Warner Brothers Records 1634).

What happened to Cosby in the story happened, in reality, to hundreds of people when Orson Welles' Mercury Theatre presented the 1938 broadcast of THE WAR OF THE WORLDS.

"Tune in again next week—same time,
same station . . ."

—an old radio

How much Jello was smeared and how many
sofas were burned on that particular night
has not, to my knowledge, been reported
in the many studies of that phenomenal incident.

All this is, of course, air waves under the bridge,
but it does seem worth mentioning in terms of
the development of our popular culture.
An authoritative reference book on the
bygone era is Jim Harmon's **The Great
Radio Heroes** (Doubleday/Ace Books), which
features numerous nostalgic anecdotes, excerpts
from early radio scripts, and additional
raw material of American mythology.

WILD BUNCH
SHOW
7 AND 9

NO PARKING

"They walked downtown in the light of
mother-of-pearl, to the Majestic, and found their
way to seats by the light of the screen, in
the exhilarating smell of stale tobacco,
rank sweat, perfume and dirty drawers, while
the piano played fast music and galloping
horses raised a grandiose flag of dust. And
there was William S. Hart with both guns
blazing and his long, horse face and his long,
hard lip, and the great country rode away
behind him as wide as the world. Then he
made a bashful face at the girl and his horse
raised its upper lip and everybody laughed,
and then the screen was filled with a city
and with the sidewalk of a side street of
a city, a long line of palms and there was
Charlie; everyone laughed the minute they
saw him squattily walking with his toes out
and knees wide apart . . ."

—James Agee, from **A Death in the Family**

THE PICTURE SHOWS

films & movies

We used to call them movies. Now, we call them films. My grandmother always calls them picture shows.

Picture shows began as magic trickery.
Movies put pop lit. on the screen.
Films aspire to art.

After more than fifty years, film has acquired sufficient cultural accreditation to grant it probationary eligibility as an art form. The increasing brouhaha about "film art" during the last decade has even qualified film for consideration in the classroom. But to talk about "film" is to talk about Antonioni, Bergman, Bunuel, Fellini, Godard and Truffaut. To talk about "movies" is something else altogether.

The movies are still with us, film art or no, and many of the new movies are—as the promo slogan says—"better than ever." Outside of the classroom, few if any of my kids have ever seen a Fellini film, but most of them saw BONNIE AND CLYDE, THE GRADUATE, 2001, EASY RIDER, BUTCH CASSIDY & THE SUNDANCE KID, or M*A*S*H. So once again, it is a matter of going with the grain, and in terms of movies, the grain has been pretty good lately. The best of the new movies teeter on the brink between art and kitsch.

"I think it's a strange mistake to take the kind of work I do seriously, to think of it as important or lasting. Plays are forgotten. Film crumbles. We all tend to make the mistake of thinking film is forever."

—Mike Nichols

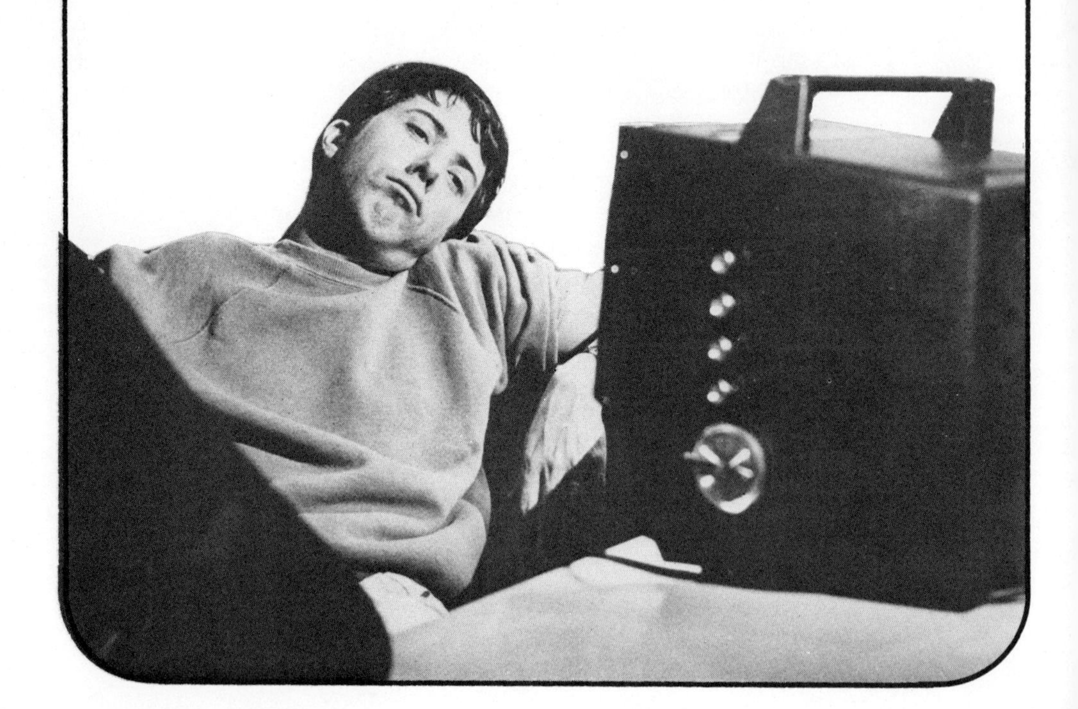

Most movies do not wear well for they are seldom concerned with universal verities, but rather with what Robert Warshow called "the immediate experience."

Not long ago, I watched James Dean in REBEL WITHOUT A CAUSE on the late, late show. When I first saw it in high school, it was THE GRADUATE of its day, a movie that seemed to sum up all the frustrations of the '50s. Seen again, nearly fifteen years after its release, REBEL WITHOUT A CAUSE was a little embarrassing, but still fairly representative of the way it used to seem to be. We all grow older and the world grows older with us, but still the movies preserve our memories and provide an index by which we can measure our growth.

In creating immediate experiences, the new movies are often more honest, more meaningful, and more entertaining and thought-provoking than most of what has gone before. Some critics would not agree. Certain schools of criticism, for instance, hold the theory that film went downhill from the time that the silent screen was endowed with sound. But film criticism today is such a mixed (and mixed-up) bag that one can find some critic somewhere to support any conceivable viewpoint, even the most outrageous.

To say that "movies are better than ever" is not, of course, to say that **all** movies are better. We have seen, of late, enough crass, exploitative schlock to fill the garbage

"There is more energy, more originality, more excitement, more **art** in American kitsch like GUNGA DIN, EASY LIVING, the Rogers and Astaire pictures like SWING TIME and TOP HAT, in STRANGERS ON A TRAIN, HIS GIRL FRIDAY, THE CRIMSON PIRATE, CITIZEN KANE, THE LADY EVE, TO HAVE AND HAVE NOT, THE AFRICAN QUEEN, SINGIN' IN THE RAIN, SWEET SMELL OF SUCCESS, or more recently, THE HUSTLER, LOLITA, THE MANCHURIAN CANDIDATE, HUD, CHARADE, than in the presumed 'High Culture' of HIROSHIMA MON AMOUR, MARIENBAD, LA NOTTE, THE ECLIPSE, and the Torre Nilsson pictures. As Nabokov remarked, 'Nothing is more exhilarating than Philistine vulgarity.'"

—Pauline Kael, "Zeitgeist and Poltergeist; Or, Are Movies Going to Pieces?" in **I Lost It At The Movies**

cans of Greater Los Angeles with film reels; but it is not usually the young you find queuing up to see the latest skinflick. Instead, it is the young who most often make up the audience for the best of the new movies, and who, by virtue of their box-office power, have brought about the recent revolution in American cinema.

Television freed film. The mass-produced "formula" films, based on pop lit. myths, provided the basic ingredients for the TV series. It was no longer necessary to go out to the Bijou, Rialto, or Orpheum when pop could be pumped right into your parlor. But the young are always less inclined to stay at home. That their parents had virtually abandoned the movie palaces only made the theatres more attractive. And as Hollywood discovered the nature of its new audience, the studios found themselves forced to abandon the old, overused assembly-line approaches to their product (or else to apply the assembly lines to television production). Some new assembly lines were set up (e.g. motorcycle movies, beach-party movies, teenage-monster movies, etc.) but the new audience was not quite as easily psyched out as was the old.

Today, it is common knowledge among the movie-makers that the young buy the tickets, but few of the movie-makers know how to sell the new market. Hollywood suffers from the delusion that "youth movies" must be movies

"Any movie that attempts honestly and maturely to come to grips with life is going to raise questions. It is going to deal with a theme worth thinking about . . ."

—William Kuhns &
Robert Stanley
Exploring the Film

about youth, and so we are treated to trumped-up tripe like Roger Corman's THE TRIP or Stuart Hagmann's THE STRAWBERRY STATEMENT—movies that purport to deal with youth issues, and turn out to be cop-outs (non-statements), rip-offs (plagiarism), or put-ons (pretension), and mainly, cash-ins.

And yet the most successful films among the new audience of the past few years have most often been those that have made strong personal statements, those that have presented important ideas, and those that have dealt honestly with life and the way we live it, regardless of the ages of the actors.

The young audience is demanding a near reversal of the old Hollywood pop mythology, which, through overexposure, they are starting to recognize as insipid and inane. Many of the most popular recent movies have been based on anti-myths (e.g., THE GRADUATE, MIDNIGHT COWBOY) or, at least, counter-myths more appropriate to the times (e.g. EASY RIDER, BONNIE AND CLYDE).

Demythologizing the movies is a task which Hollywood is ill-prepared to undertake. The transition from vending comfortable cliches to making movies that matter is causing tremendous growth pains in the movie industry. In fact, the pains will probably prove

"I was raised
On matinees
On Saturday afternoons
Looking up at Hoppy, Gene, & Roy
And I grew up a-thinking
The best a man can do
Is to be a Rootin' Tootin'
Straight Shootin'
Cowboy Buckaroo"

—Mason Williams,
COWBOY BUCKAROO

fatal to the old Hollywood system. Still, the best always tends to endure; Hollywood has produced some of the best in pop entertainment. The new screen scene also promises to produce some excellent entertainment and maybe even something more.

Prior to the 1969 Academy Awards presentations, **Life** magazine featured an article contrasting the two leading contenders for the "Best Actor" oscar—John Wayne for his role as Rooster Cogburn in TRUE GRIT, and Dustin Hoffman for his portrayal of Ratso Rizzo in MIDNIGHT COWBOY. For examples of the changing screen, **Life** could scarcely have made a better selection of symbols.

John Wayne's climactic gunfight in TRUE GRIT somehow captured the essence of every western from THE GREAT TRAIN ROBBERY to A FISTFUL OF DOLLARS. It is a synopsis of all the myth and legend that made the movies the most popular of our popular arts. And as Hollywood prepares to say goodbye to all that, it is only natural that the award go to the one star who best represents the passing of that era. Thespian talents have nothing to do with it. John Wayne is a superstar, an image of the mythic America. Dustin Hoffman is merely a fine actor.

"Really, it is not violence at all which is the 'point' of the Western movie, but a certain image of man, a style, which expresses itself most clearly in violence. Watch a child with his toy guns and you will see: what most interests him is not (as we so much fear) the fantasy of hurting others, but to work out how a man might look when he shoots or is shot. A hero is one who looks like a hero."

—Robert Warshow, "Movie Chronicle: The Westerner" in **The Immediate Experience**

The Great American Double Feature of recent years would have to be TRUE GRIT and MIDNIGHT COWBOY*, run in tandem so as to appear to be one continuous film.

Fade out as John Wayne rides off with leathery bravado, and cut to the blank screen of the West Texas drive-in theatre with the ghostly soundtrack of thundering hooves and the echoes of gunfire. Joe Buck, the Midnight Cowboy, is a young, would-be John Wayne gone bad, forever overshadowed by the archetypal image, and hopelessly stranded in the 20th century without a range to ride.

MIDNIGHT COWBOY is a movie about movies, and about what might happen to the hapless yo-yo who takes the popular culture at its word. That few kids were able to see it—due to its "x" rating—is, I believe, an unfortunate example of misguided moralism, because MIDNIGHT COWBOY is what the new movies—their movies—are all about.

In the new movies, stars are giving way to actors, the studio/producer is giving way to the author/director, and myth is gradually giving way to "truth—at 24 frames-per-second."

*The runner-up for Great American Double-Feature would be PATTON and M*A*S*H. The combination of BENEATH THE PLANET OF THE APES and BEYOND THE VALLEY OF THE DOLLS was not in the running.

"Rooster said, 'I mean to kill you in one minute, Ned, or see you hanged in Fort Smith at Judge Parker's convenience! Which will you have?'

"Lucky Ned Pepper laughed. He said, 'I call that bold talk for a one-eyed fat man!'

"Rooster said, 'Fill your hand, you son of a bitch!' and he took the reins in his teeth and pulled the other saddle revolver and drove his spurs into the flanks of his strong horse Bo and charged directly at the bandits. It was a sight to see."

—Charles Portis, **True Grit**

"This day in late September marked the beginning of Joe Buck's alliance with Ratso Rizzo. The pair of them became a familiar sight on certain New York streets that fall, the little blond runt, laboring like a broken grasshopper to keep pace with the six-foot tarnished cowboy, the two of them frowning their way through time like children with salt shakers stalking a bird, urgently intent on their task of finding something of worth in the streets of Manhattan."

—James Leo Herlihy,
Midnight Cowboy

"Different strokes for different folks . . ."
—folk saying, popularized by
Sly & The Family Stone

"Truth at 24-frames-per-second" still takes it on the chin now and then, a notable example being the uncanny success of LOVE STORY, a throwback which included all the sentimental cliches ever invented, and still attracted crowds of ticket buyers, young and old, and all apparently prone to easy emotional catharsis.

Time magazine and others to the contrary, it seems a dubious proposition that the success of LOVE STORY heralds a new Romantic Movement in cinema and society. (The comparable financial success of THE SOUND OF MUSIC, for example, evidently did not inspire the return of mushy musicals.) There is a distinction to be made between Romanticism and Sentimentalism. For a study in that contrast, the Great American Double Feature might be LOVE STORY and Bob Rafelson's FIVE EASY PIECES, a truly romantic film of some depth and substance.

The differences between Jack Nicholson's Bobby Eroica Dupea and Karen Black's Rayette DiPesto as opposed to Ryan O'Neil's Oliver Barrett IV and Ali MacGraw's Jennifer Cavilleri are as enormous as the differences between flesh and blood human beings and Ken and Barbie dolls.

To paraphrase Oscar Wilde's epigrammatic assault on Dickens, it takes a heart of stone to see or read of the death of Jennifer Cavilleri without laughing. On the other hand, it is doubtful that the most caustic cynic could remain unmoved by Bobby Dupea's farewell to his father.

As movies go, FIVE EASY PIECES is the creme de la creme. LOVE STORY is pure canned corn. As time goes by, maybe we can at least hope for a growing preponderance of creamed corn.

"Speaking in the large, I believe that the Film Generation has the power to evoke the films that it wants, even though that generation is a minority and despite the harsh conditions of production and exhibition around the world. **All** films will not alter, nor should they, but if the dynamics of cultural history still obtains, an insistent group of art takers can—sooner or later, one way or another—have an effect on art makers. The effect is circular. The audience obviously cannot do it alone; there have to be talented artists. But talent is a relative constant in the human race; it is sparked by response and, even at its best, can be dampened by neglect."

—Stanley Kauffmann,
"The Film Generation"
in **A World On Film**

More and more is being written about what critic Stanley Kauffmann calls "The Film Generation." Hundreds of colleges have added film study courses to their curricula, and many inroads have been made into bringing film study to the high school, junior high, and even elementary school—not as "audio-visual aids"—but as a subject of study.

With its tortoise-like speed, education has finally deigned to direct some attention to a communication medium which has been a part of American life for more than half-a-century; and this is often thought to be a "progressive" idea.

Why the delay? Probably, in part, because the moralism of the movies is quite different from that of the schools. Puritan morality is as ingrained in education as it is in our society at large. In terms of movies, it was always a superimposition. For years, the movies got away with murder, so to speak, by simply tagging on a "moral of the story." Only recently have films begun to abandon this hypocrisy. Education may never abandon it, although it is reasonably clear that all life experiences cannot be easily interpreted as moral parable.

As was the case with comic books, Forces for Good in the Community advocate the merits of "good clean fun" (read: pure fantasy in which all references to the

"He was MR. CLEAN now. All reference to him as a serious film artist had long since ceased and in a period when traditional middle-class values—indeed, the traditional middle class itself—were being questioned as they had not been since the 1920s, Walt Disney became, in the minds of his public, something more than a purveyor of entertainment. He became a kind of rallying point for the subliterates of our society, the chosen leader of the desultory—and ambiguous—rear-guard action they were trying to fight against a rapidly changing cultural climate."

—Richard Schickel,
The Disney Version

realities of life, love, and death are carefully filtered out). The name of Walt Disney is invariably intoned.

The new audience, on the other hand, calls for an end to sham and censorship, and the freedom that will allow film to fulfill its potential.

Dealing honestly with the subject matter of life, love, and death has never been the forte of either education or the movies. But the movies, for all their fantasy and mythology, often seemed somewhat closer to what life is all about than did education, where life is all too frequently reduced to something to be measured, recorded, and studied from afar, but not quite lived. In school we are taught to behave ourselves and conform to the norm. The movies always offer more exciting alternatives.

From the first, the vested interests of education took to disdaining and condemning that glamorous appeal with which they could not compete. Education resorted to the "cultural" cop-out: the aesthetic and literary crudity of the movies, like that of all popular arts, was held to be beneath the contempt of the serious scholar. Still and all, even the serious scholar has been known to sneak off to the picture shows on occasion.

"If you don't think movies can be killed, you underestimate the power of education."
—Pauline Kael

Now, at last, we have come to the point where movies (and the other media) assert such a pervasive influence on our lives that even education can no longer completely ignore them. It has been decided that some of those flickering images just might be art, and therefore, we must teach our children to "appreciate" them as we have taught them to "appreciate" literature, music, painting, and all the other arts.

I, for one (Pauline Kael for another), deplore that idea. It is not that I disagree that films can be art, but rather that I have serious reservations about the abilities of educators to deal with them as such. Art can take care of itself. It educates in its own way, in its own time. Our task, as I see it, is not to attempt to murder film as we have the other seven once-lively arts, but rather to use film, movies, the other media, as mirrors to help us find out who we are, what we are, where we are, and what we can do about it.

Old Warner Pathe newsreels used to bear the slogan—"The Eyes and Ears of the World"—and though the newsreels have been replaced by David Brinkley and Walter Cronkite, that slogan lingers on, for film and TV are indeed the eyes and ears of the world (and all the other senses, too, according to Professor McLuhan), showing us ourselves through a lens darkly.

"The movies are one of the bad habits that corrupted our century."

—Ben Hecht.* **A Child Of The Century**

*NOTE: Mr. Hecht's early life and career served as the basis for the motion picture. GAILY, GAILY.

The picture shows are mirrors of our life
and time, and even if, as in the amusement
park fun house mirrors, the reflection is
a bit distorted, it is a recognizable image
nonetheless.

For the first time in human history, man
has the ability to watch "instant replays"
of his glories and follies, his victories and
defeats, his heroism and his stupidity.
That ability should be used to help us learn.

What do the films of the future have in
store for us?

In the light of recent technical developments,
it seems probable that we will, one day soon,
be able to buy film cartridges or cassettes for
private home projection just as we now buy
books, records, or tapes. This eventuality
would put an end to many of the limitations now
imposed on films for public performance.
What would be available would be even
more contingent on consumer demands.

Also, some breakthroughs in the production
of inexpensive movie-making equipment may
make it feasible for films of the future to be
produced by individuals for mass distribution,
putting the filmmaker in a situation similar to
that of the novelist. Home movies are probably
the harbingers of new modes of creative
expression, hard as that may be to believe for
those of us who have sat through OUR TRIP TO
YELLOWSTONE PARK or BABY'S FIRST
BIRTHDAY.

"New directions are being opened up by American film makers. Reaching for specific intensities of existence, they are taking the materials of electronic technology and making new images. And the sense of different ways of being alive becomes the theme."

—advertisement brochure for
THE KINETIC ART Series 2

In terms of changing themes and content, much of the experimental, avant-garde, and "underground" cinema seems hung up on overreacting to traditional taboos (e.g., the treatment of sex in movies having been Puritanical in the past, we are now besieged by nudie movies, which often seem terribly inhibited in their struggle to be uninhibited). That phase, I assume, will eventually pass.

The best new techniques from the underground are usually assimilated quickly and adapted to the more conventional narrative structure of theatrical films. We have also begun to see the emergence of what might be termed the "overground-underground" in feature films like John Cassavetes' FACES, Robert Downey's PUTNEY SWOPE, and Brian De Palma's GREETINGS and HI, MOM.

New efforts in both narrative forms and non-narrative visual experiences are to be found in experimental short films such as those included in the NEW CINEMA collection (Janus/Pyramid) and the KINETIC ART series (Universal).

Innovation is also apparent in some of the student films, although one must usually endure hours of sophomoric footage to see a few minutes of original ideas. The experience is comparable to reading Creative Writing compositions.

"How could we possibly appreciate the Mona Lisa if Leonardo had written at the bottom of the canvas: 'The lady is smiling because she is hiding a secret from her lover.' This would shackle the viewer to reality, and I don't want this to happen to **2001.**"

—Stanley Kubrick, in **The Making of Kubrick's 2001,** edited by Jerome Agel

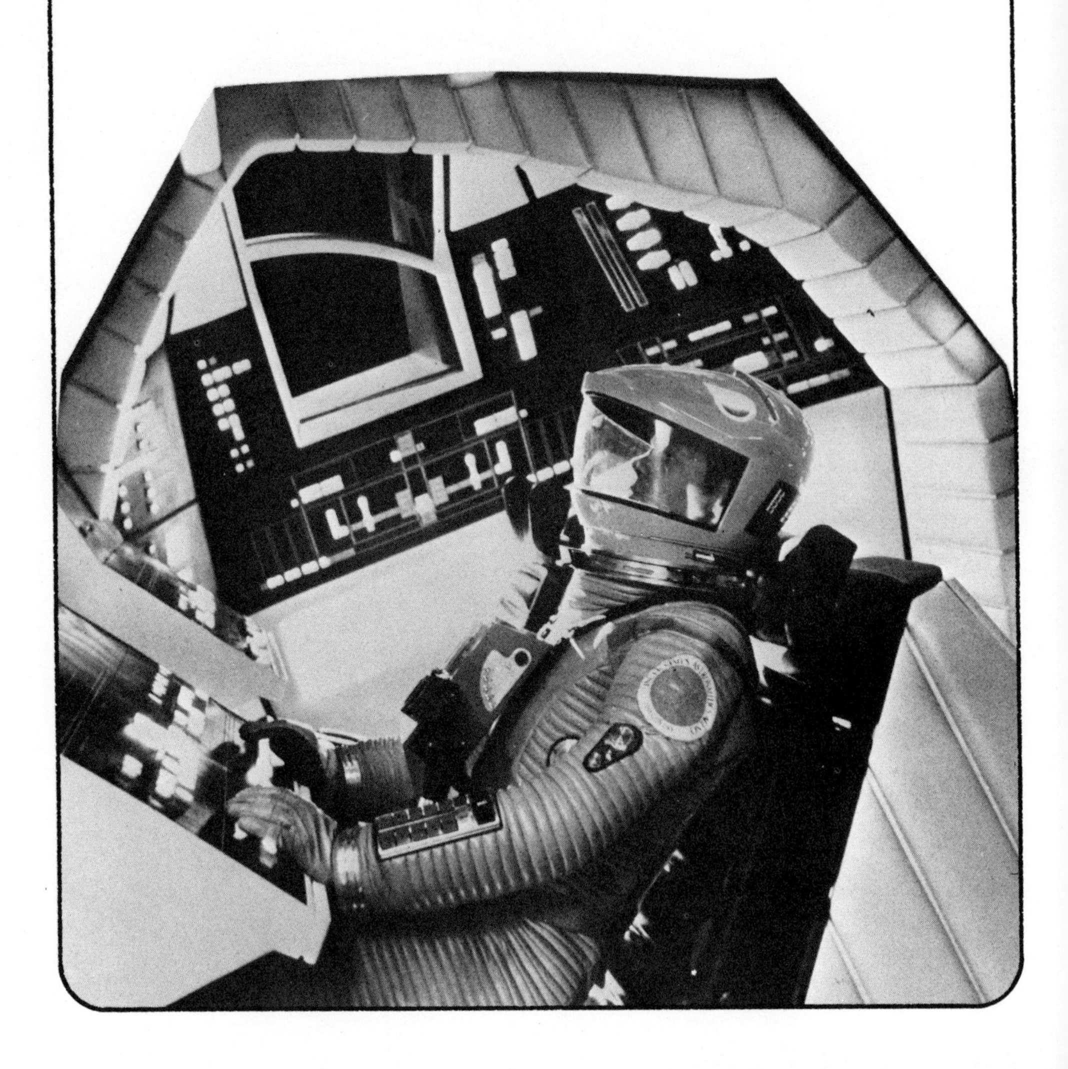

I would guess that one likely precursor of films to come would be Stanley Kubrick's 2001: A SPACE ODYSSEY. 2001 might well become this generation's GONE WITH THE WIND. It is a futuristic film in both form and content. It can be viewed on several levels—as spectacular science fiction entertainment, as an enthralling visual experience, as social commentary, or as metaphysical metaphor. Director Kubrick has been, and continues to be, a pioneer of the new movies with such diversified and groundbreaking accomplishments as PATHS OF GLORY, LOLITA, and DR. STRANGELOVE to his credit. His approach to film is as individualistic as any to be found in the underground, and his technical skills reflect a mastery of all that motion pictures have been as well as what they might become.

If current trends continue, we are also likely to see an increase in the low-budget, highly personalized film, which features a mixture of fictional and documentary modes (sort of a cinema semi-verite). Dennis Hopper's EASY RIDER, Haskell Wexler's MEDIUM COOL, and the films of Jean-Luc Godard give early indications of this new direction. This approach emphasizes the idea of film as reality perceived by the director. It is as close as film (which is essentially a group effort by producer, director, writer, cameraman, actors, editor) can come to the one-man show. After the fashion of the Europeans, the American director is coming into his own as the **auteur,** whose signature is

"I have seen a great many bad movies,
and I know when a movie is bad, but I have
rarely been bored at the movies; and when
I have been bored, it has usually been at a
'good' movie."

—Robert Warshow, preface to
The Immediate Experience

writ large on his film, supplanting the rubber stamp of the studio.

Above all, entertainment is bound to endure during the future of film, for film is a mass medium first, an art second. It is frequently repeated that the mass media are aimed at "the lowest common denominator." Whether or not we can create a higher common denominator depends partly on education.

Simply to rail against the mediocre and mundane will not do the trick. Such an attitude is generally humorless, and neither convincing nor constructive.

If the kids are flocking to the local drive-in to see WILD ANGELS or NIGHT OF THE LIVING DEAD or A FISTFUL OF DOLLARS, then that is the place to begin. These films may be considered unaesthetic or even appalling to "refined tastes," but in their own way, they reflect some of the same themes that show up in Antonioni's L'AVVENTURA or Fellini's LA DOLCE VITA. If we are really to teach film, we must learn to teach The Good, The Bad, and The Ugly.

Within the limits of one part of one chapter of one book on a general survey of mass media and popular culture, it is, of course, impossible to present a thoroughgoing critical evaluation of the new American cinema. At any rate,

"Films are to be viewed, not reviewed."
—an Electric Humanities
student

such criticism is already rampant and readily available for further research. The sources mentioned here are, to my mind, some of the best and most valuable to the prospective film teacher. But the most valuable resource of all is still the screen itself. It is infinitely preferable to see the movies for yourself, as opposed to reading reviews and criticism. Then, **with your students,** come to your own conclusions, come up with your own critiques. They will prove to be the most valuable of all.

"I mean it's real hard to be free when you are bought and sold in the marketplace."
—Jack Nicholson as
George in EASY RIDER

"Film is an art-form, an expensive art-form, it's the Sistine Chapel of the Twentieth Century, it's the best way to reach people."

—Dennis Hopper, "Into the Issue of the Good Old Time Movie Versus the Good Old Time"

"If it moves, the public will watch it."
—Marvin Kitman, **You Can't Judge a Book By Its Cover**

the tube

Newton Minow called it "the vast wasteland." Harlan Ellison calls it "the glass teat." Mason Williams calls it "an electronic medicine show." Marshall McLuhan calls it "a cool medium," "a mosaic mesh," "an extension of the sense of touch, which involves maximal interplay of all the senses." Most of us call it "television."

There is a main criticism made of television, the same criticism made of the "underachieving" student: "You have the abilities if only you would apply yourself."

Television is, without a doubt, the All-Time Underachiever. Its potential to inform, entertain, and educate is unquestionable. How that potential is applied is obvious to anyone who has ever watched the NEWS, WEATHER, & SPORTS, the ED SULLIVAN SHOW, or HABLAMOS EN ESPANOL.

There are moments of glory, of course, but moments within years are diminished in significance.

Such carping, I know, is contradictory to my basic thesis ("Simply to rail against the mediocre and mundane will not do the trick."), but neither paperback print nor the movies ever held quite the promise of television. To date, it is a broken promise.

"Television is an instrument, like a telephone, that can be used when wanted. It may not be wanted for six days and nights of the week, but on the seventh it may provide something which no other instrument, no other medium, can provide."

—Marya Mannes, "The Lost Tribe of Television" in **The Eighth Art**

Perhaps, like the movies, television will
require a space of time to grow and evolve.
If it would be at all possible to hasten television
evolution through education, we should
definitely get it on; yet TV has felt the
embrace of education, and if ETV is the child of
that union, maybe we should leave well enough
alone.

My own discouragement with television is not
meant to imply that, in regard to this one
medium, I share the convictions of the Cultural
Mafia. I do not. I see no prospect for prime-time
Shakespeare Festivals, or classical concerts with
high scores on the Nielsen ratings. Television,
like all mass media, is now and evermore shall
be, by and large, a vehicle for popular culture.
It is the poverty of pop on TV which distresses
me. With few exceptions, television pop
strikes me as unimaginative, decidedly
plagiaristic, and often dishonest past the point
of mythologizing. In short, it is usually low-grade
schmaltz—unoriginal and uninteresting. Good,
honest pop entertainment, on a par with the
best of movies, paperbacks, and old radio, would
be one small step for television but a giant leap
for popular culture. Perhaps even that is
asking too much.

After all, maybe the medium is the message;
maybe the mere "comforting presence" of the
tube is all we can expect of it; maybe it is
enough to have our awareness extended

"TV programming can be creative, educational, uplifting, and refreshing without being tedious. But the current television product that drains away lifetimes of leisure energy is none of these. It leaves its addicts waterlogged. Only rarely does it contribute anything meaningful to their lives."

—F.C.C. Commissioner
Nicholas Johnson.

"No one should have illusions about television. It is **never** going to be primarily an educational and cultural medium."

—Eric Sevareid

throughout the global village, now and again, enabling us to keep up on, if not cope with, all the current crises; maybe . . .

Let us cast a jaundiced, critical eye at the stuff of television once again, and try to come up with some test patterns for teaching TV. One thing is sure: Ignoring it won't make it go away.

First of all, we have television as entertainment—Electronic Melodrama.

At present, much of TV is old movies, both literally and figuratively—old movies, movies-for-television (new old movies), and that standard fare, the TV series (short new old movies). The TV series is the heir apparent to our popular mythology; if pop myths can be bastardized, TV can do it. The reason for the predominance of poor pop on the tube has doubtless to do with the quantitative factor. Filling TV time requires the same kind of assembly lines perfected by Hollywood in its pre-TV heyday. Thus did many of the major movie studios sell out to their competition out of economic necessity, peddling their old formulae for mass entertainment. Neither popular print nor motion pictures ever made such demands for prolific production. Budd Schulberg's Sammy Glick would have to run a whole lot faster to win in the TV writing rat race.

"In the first thirty seconds the pilot should go like this, 'Fifty thousand murderous Berbers are headed toward Cairo, and only you, Dick Daring, can stop them.' Dick Daring, that's our hero . . ."

—network executive explains the essence of a TV series to writer Merle Miller in **Only You, Dick Daring!**

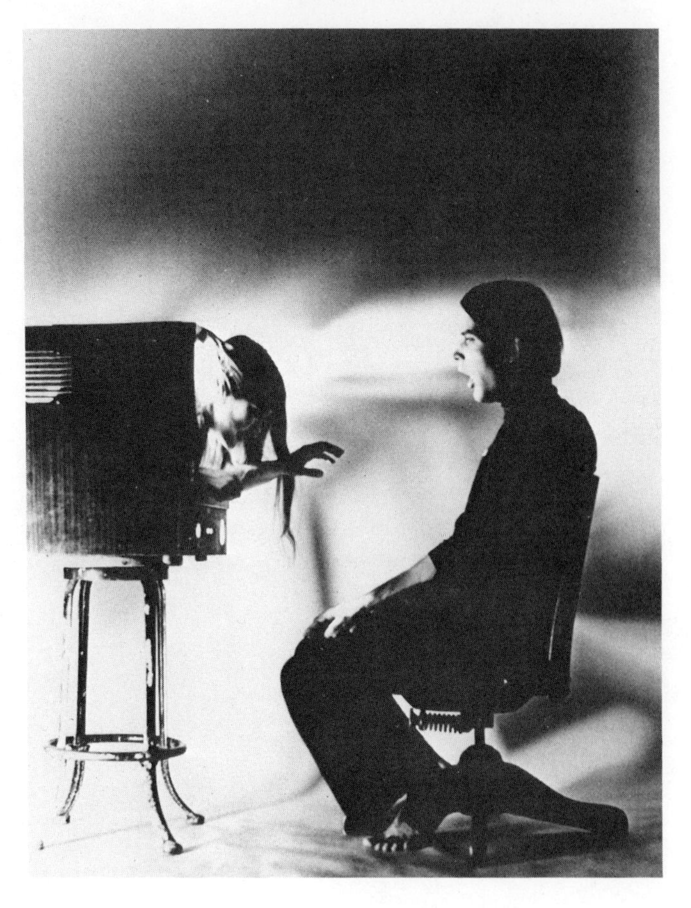

An aside: It was once my displeasure to be enrolled in a college class called "Experimental Methods in TV Writing," sponsored by a major television network which shall remain unnamed. The avowed purpose of the course was to discover "new talent" for the TV industry. Those of us involved—all graduate students—were told that this would be our golden opportunity to upgrade TV entertainment. As it turned out, the "experimental methods" amounted to writing scripts from provided story lines for TV series shows which had already been produced. The measure of a "good" script was its similarity to the show as scripted by the network cliche-mongers. So much for experimental TV at the network level.

Since that time, I have had occasion to chat with several professional TV writers, who seem to be mostly cynical chaps with commitments to cash, chips on their shoulders, and compromised talents. That they can stay in a system that chews up and spits out its contributors at such a rapid rate speaks well, at least, for their endurance.

I refer disbelievers in the foregoing anecdotes to the experience of Merle Miller as cleverly chronicled in **Only You. Dick Daring!** by Miller and Evan Rhodes.

The balance of TV entertainment consists mostly of the musical-comedy-variety shows—Electronic Vaudeville.

"We use a cheap trick in writing the Smothers Brothers show. We simply write things that have meaning. It's an area just laying there that no other variety show in television is using."

—Mason Williams (Sept., '68),
The Mason Williams F.C.C. Rapport

Everyone has surely seen Sullivan, Dean Martin, Glenn Campbell, Tom Jones, whoever. Why elaborate? What is there to say?

The defunct SMOTHERS BROTHERS COMEDY HOUR provided a few occasionally interesting variations on the theme, thanks to the offbeat talents of its stars, material by writer Mason Williams, and some good guest performers from outside the regular variety show circuit. But the Smothers Brothers hardly broke the mold. They only bent it a little bit. That their hassles with network censors (resulting in the show's eventual cancellation) should cause such widespread publicity and controversy only demonstrates how deeply entrenched the formulated format has become.

Another show—ROWAN & MARTIN'S LAUGH-IN—was also something of a mold bender in the beginning with its breakneck bombardment of blackout humor and its visual innovations, but as is the wont of the wonderful world of television, a new format having been found, it was quickly beaten into another overworked formula.

Unavoidable conclusion on TV entertainment: We watch a lot of baloney. We are told, by the rating surveys, that we like the baloney. The world is tough enough without a screenful of reminders. We all have to get away from it once in a while, and at least TV entertainment

"One can spend infinite hours worrying about what to do with and how to fix television, when perhaps, as a soothing narcotic of sorts, it is just what the doctor ordered to calm down the super-charged American. The minority of our people will continue to rely on books, well-done movies, and carefully selected drama and music for cultural enrichment. And the majority will wallow joyfully with Joanna Barnes, 'Beverly Hillbillies,' 'Days of Our Lives,' and Virginia Graham. The majority seems happy—or at least not actively unhappy—with television as it is. The minority grouses and I suppose will continue to grouse about the quality of this ravenous medium. Maybe it is time for the minority to quit devouring itself in its continual orgy of critical scrutiny, to say the hell with it, **caveat emptor,** and go its own way."

—Charles Sopkin,
Seven Glorious Days.
Seven Fun-Filled Nights

is comparatively safer than dope or alcohol. To watch a little baloney is no crime at all. To **believe** in it verges on idiocy. Maybe the best we can do is to teach kids how to take TV or leave it alone.

Television critic Charles Sopkin undertook an ordeal **above and** beyond the call of duty, when he spent a solid week watching six TV sets simultaneously (separate channels), sign on to sign off. After his "seven glorious days, seven fun-filled nights," he concluded: "I naively expected that the ratio would run three to one in favor of trash. It turned out to be closer to a hundred to one," and "My frank opinion now is that there is **no** way to make television better. It is what it is."

Secondly, we have television as information —the Electronic Newspaper.

Vice President Agnew and some others to the contrary, television has earned some well-deserved acclaim for its news coverage. In its reportage function, as nowhere else, TV demonstrates its potential for greatness. But, asks Mason Williams, "Isn't it fantastic that everything that happens every day is exactly an hour's worth of news?"

Who decides what news should be shown and what should be edited out?

"Strangely, the greatest moments of television news have occurred when the camera simply has been turned on to watch an event in progress, when the news department's function of choice and condensation has been exercised to a minimum, or not at all."

—Walter Cronkite, "Television and News" in **The Eighth Art**

Is TV journalism objective? Is objectivity possible?

A newsfilm camera, in the midst of an event, must focus on specific scenes. As is also the case with human perception, it is impossible to take in everything that is happening.

Perhaps the focus is on the protester as he hurls the rock through the plate glass window. The camera cannot report on the motives behind the act, the validity of his grievance, the chain of personal experiences that lead to that moment. It only reports the rock, the shattered glass, the act of outrage.

Perhaps the focus is on the cop as he clubs the demonstrator, not showing a previous moment when the cop was hit with a brick or a broken bottle.

The camera reports the political speeches, the exodus of refugees, the fire fight, the body count. It cannot reveal the wheels within wheels, the wherefore and the why . . .

Of all the thousands of feet of newsfilm shot each day, someone somewhere must pick and choose what he sees as the representative scenes of the selected stories. The news comes to us filtered through the cameraman, the editor, the production staff,

"In this year of decision, the world is watching America; America is watching TV."
—**The Farmer's Almanac**

"THE WHOLE WORLD IS WATCHING!"
—demonstrators' chant in Chicago, 1968

the newscaster, and others all along the line. We are left to view the dramatic daily events, and to fill in the gaps with our own imaginations, opinions, and prejudices.

"You can't believe everything you read in the papers." You can't believe everything you see on the tube.

Those on the right will say the news is leaning toward the left. Those on the left will accuse it of leaning to the right. Those who gather and report the news will say they walk the line, the middle of the road.

The questions concerning TV journalism are of critical importance. Are "the eyes and ears of the world" partially impaired? If so, how can the impairment be corrected?

Can the whole truth be told on TV? If not, what effects will half-truths have?

Can TV, in the name of news, be made the pawn of partisan causes from guerilla street theatre to political campaigns?

It's time we learned to read the news, be it print or pictures.

Next, we have TV as education—
the Electronic Textbook.

"It's not that I'm against Educational TV. (I mean, how can one be against Educational TV?) But people tend to have these rather automatic ideas about it—that anything informative is therefore educational, and that anything educational is therefore good—with the result that most of the programs I've watched on Channel 13, the local Educational TV station, seem to exist in a sort of sacred vacuum in which the producers and the viewers are so busy admiring the high-minded purity of each other's motives that it often seems that one could film thirty minutes of a seventh-grade geography class and title it 'New Horizons in Geography' and Channel 13 would run it and people would sit before their sets fairly glowing with enrichment."

—Michael J. Arlen,
The Living-Room War

Education already does a less than adequate job in the personal, face-to-face, environment of the classroom. Why it should want to broadcast its deficiencies on a mass medium is a mystery to me.

In Brian De Palma's film, HI, MOM, ETV is caricatured as "NIT" ("National Intellectual Television")—TV of the intellectual, for the intellectual, and by the intellectual. Now, presumably the intellectual already has a basic education. Why, then, should so much of ETV be directed at him?

Because he's the only one who will watch it, that's why. The audience most likely to benefit from educational television seems seldom to turn it on. Why not? Because, compared to commercial television, ETV is deadly dull. Again, we have the classic paradox of entertainment as education, but not vice-versa.

In all fairness to ETV, there has been some progress from the televised lectures and panel discussions of its early years. It has moved more in the direction of documentary and dramatic programming, but the documentary has never been the most popular program of the medium, and in terms of drama, the TV ratings assure us that BONANZA will outdraw Bernard Shaw every time. The missing ingredient in ETV is obviously popular appeal.

"There is no reason why what is considered to be Cultural and educational cannot be developed into solidly entertaining formats that attract the large audiences that are necessary to sustain commercial television; nor is there any reason why the techniques of mass entertainment cannot be harnessed to make Cultural and educational television fare far more palatable than it has been or is right now."

—Harold Mendelsohn,
Mass Entertainment

Another aside: Not long ago, in Denver, Colorado, an interesting experiment was undertaken in which the local educational channel produced a series of "soap operas" with built-in social messages and no soap. Within the context of the story line, the viewer was given information on such common problems as unemployment, discrimination, lack of education, etc., as well as information on the various social agencies available for help with such problems. The information was injected almost incidentally as the show's cast of characters attempted to cope with the problems personally. Such entertainment/education combinations as this would seem to indicate at least one possible new direction for TV programming to take.

The success of NET's widely acclaimed SESAME STREET reinforces the validity of the education-as-entertainment approach. What is needed now is a SESAME STREET for adults.

Considering the high costs of television and the limited budgets allotted to ETV, it is, of course, hard pressed to compete with its commercial counterparts, and yet the one factor in its favor is its freedom to experiment without worrying about the ratings that dictate to commercial TV. Experimentation is the only way to better television; it has to start somewhere. If ETV fails to take appropriate advantage of its creative freedom, so much the worse for all of us.

Finally, we have television as advertising —The Electronic Con-Job.

"Television is not a salesman with his foot in your door, it's a salesman with his foot in your head."

—Mason Williams, **The F.C.C. Rapport**

This takes us back to some of the basic ideas mentioned in the Electric Environment. It is common knowledge and common criticism that television and advertising are inseparable, that sponsors are responsible for TV content, that "the business of television is business" (to paraphrase Calvin Coolidge).

To have at hand the most powerful communications medium of all time, and to use it to sell used cars, cosmetics, and beer is not only reprehensible—it is totally insane. To reduce the potential of television to the ludicrous level of bland, inoffensive, juvenile schlock (without even the imaginative merits of a paperback novel) in order to con consumers is despicable. To pander incessantly to the "lowest common denominator" on a medium that could possibly be arbitrating some of our most severe social problems is an outrageous crime against our whole society.

Lots of people say that.

But nobody does anything about it. It is up to us and the upcoming generation to start "talking back to our television sets," and we can begin by teaching TV in our schools.

"It has been estimated that at least 70 per cent of current box-office revenue comes from young people between the ages of sixteen and twenty-nine."

—**Saturday Review**

"By the time a typical American student graduates from high school today, he has watched more than 15,000 hours of television and has seen more than 500 films. The TV figure is the result of an average of twenty hours of weekly viewing for fifteen years, adding up to two full years of twenty-four-hours-a-day televiewing. During this same period of time, this average student has attended school five hours a day, 180 days a year, for twelve years, to produce a total of 10,800 hours of school time. Only sleeping surpasses television as the top time-consumer."

—John Culkin's famous statistics from **Film Study in the High School**

the school & the screen

In this chapter, I have tried to touch upon
some of the topics to be considered in
regard to the visual media in an Electric
Humanities survey. As previously noted,
some schools have already established
film & media study programs.

My own work in this area has indicated
that there are a great many teachers who
want to try it, but don't know where to
begin. Many times, they get hung up on
the logistics of initiating such classes—
budgetary problems involving film rental
fees, filmmaking equipment costs, textbook
purchase, etc.

As film & media study becomes another
"discipline" in an already overdisciplined
curriculum, supply problems start to take
on an unnecessary importance. All that
is really needed to teach the Electric
Humanities is an interested teacher, a bunch
of interested kids, and a place to sit and
talk. Everything else is frosting.

We all go to the movies, watch TV, listen
to the radio, read popular print. We have the
shared experiences to work with. Having already
been exposed to the media, we can, in the
classroom, proceed to compare, discuss, analyze,
criticize, investigate, and explore our media
experiences. Whenever possible, it is helpful and
enjoyable to bring new media

"The hope is that films—and today's young people's fascination with films—can illuminate something of what goes on in school, can enrich and surprise, can open up and reveal the stuff of art and life in ways which in many areas of our frozen curriculum seem to be closed off."

—David Mallery, **The School and The Art of Motion Pictures**

"At their best, films communicate valid and significant human experiences which illuminate our common humanity and which we should want to share with our students. At their worst, and they share this fault with all media, they present a dehumanizing view of man against which the best defense is trained intelligence and aesthetic judgment. The power of the moving image to manipulate, to editorialize, and to form values and attitudes makes it imperative in this age of film and television that the audience be equipped with the competence needed to understand the rhetoric of the projected image."

—John Culkin, **Film Study In The High School**

experiences into the school. It's fun and
it's worthwhile, but it isn't absolutely
necessary.

The best teachers have always done most
of their work with their own minds and
the minds of their students. These days,
it is all too easy to become enslaved to
audio-visual aids. It's always important
to remember that "aids" are all they are,
all they're supposed to be. The teacher is
still supposed to carry the weight.

My school, like most schools, is forever
without sufficient funds. Luckily, the
administration has been relatively open
to experimental ideas (prompted, in part,
by a frightening drop-out rate). My own
options were to teach the Electric Humanities
without the frills or not to teach it at all.
We had the good fortune to receive an American
Film Institute grant for the rental of a series of
feature films, and the school provided a
miniscule allowance for a paperback library of
reference books (If they'll buy you anything,
you can bet it'll be books). But even without
these books, I would opt to teach the class under
any circumstances. I think it is important.

Thus far, there has been no shortage of students
willing to elect the Electric Humanities,
and their contributions to

"The place of film study in a liberal arts education may be somewhat precarious, but its continued presence seems assured. The dialogue between those who teach the history, criticism, and appreciation of motion pictures is certain to continue in further symposia and conferences. The question of **whether** to teach motion pictures has been resolved affirmatively. The question of **how,** while it will never be answered to everyone's (perhaps **any**one's) satisfaction, found the beginning of a definition in Professor (Jack C.) Ellis' comment, 'With such a rich medium, there is more than enough to go around. As long as it is taught with affection and respect, almost any approach can increase understanding and appreciation.'"

—David C. Stewart, **Film Study in Higher Education**

the development of the class have helped to expand and enhance the original idea. Within the general framework outlined here, it has always been student interests which have given the Electric Humanities its impetus and direction.

At the present time, there are two basic approaches to film & media study: the active and the passive.

The active approach talks about the "languages" of film and TV, and learning the "grammar" thereof. This approach often involves a study of film history and techniques, and usually involves actual student filmmaking. Reportedly, it has been highly successful in all types of schools, with all kinds of kids. Active involvement in the filmmaking process is said to give students an awareness of the fundamentals of perception, some basic technical skills in photography, some insight into professional filmmaking, and an outlet for creative energy.

I believe that it probably does all that in most cases, the one problem being that the approach is much more costly than, say, creative writing or arts & crafts.

The other problem being that it is extremely easy to get kids hooked on film. For every filmmaking class, you are likely to have, at least, two or three devoted

"As the reel revolves, the film involves.
Film illuminates more than the screen.
It can make the name of the game . . .
excitement. Film study cannot succeed
without the teacher's energy and
imagination, his patience and research.
In other words, it must begin with you."

—David A. Sohn, **Film Study and The English Teacher**

"Clearly the impact of the moving image on
society is a phenomenon of our times and the
indisputable truth is that we know little of
its effects and give sparse attention to
understanding and guiding the relationship
between films and audience . . . It is my belief
that the answer lies not in censorship, but
in education. It seems to me that the solution
should not be to stifle or limit this remarkable
medium, but to make film the subject of study
and to provide the users, particularly the
younger ones, with a film education which
will make them discriminating viewers. The
very process will enlarge knowledge about the
effects of these media and provide an audience
which will inspire, nourish and support
filmmakers of the future."

—George Stevens, Jr., Director of the American Film Institute, introductory remarks at the AFI Leadership Conference: On Teaching the Film, 1968

disciples who will decide, on the basis
of the success of their 8mm. movies, to
pursue a career in filmmaking; it will be
those kids who will be joining the throngs
already storming the gates of every existing
college film department. Of all the students
graduating with degrees in film & media, only a
small percentage have any hope of actually
making a living as filmmakers. Sad but true.

A suggestion: Since the passion for film & media
seems unlikely to subside in the near future,
a remedial action on the part of the colleges
and universities might be the development of
programs to channel some of the interest into
related areas like film & media criticism,
teaching, or research.

My own allegiance is to the passive approach,
and what the American Film Institute refers
to as "audience development." In general,
we seem to be much more in need of a
discerning audience than we are of more
unemployed underground filmmakers. I have
never been altogether convinced about
the validity of studying film per se, despite the
fact that it is an admittedly attractive pastime.

The socio-psycho-anthropo-passive approach
of the Electric Humanities—the study of
media as mirrors and mythology—seems to
me to be a little more pragmatic. Its

"We would do well to remember that we are already educating the citizens of 1984: also that, for them, the 1960s will perhaps have as much an air of antiquity as have the 1660s for us.

"The challenge to educators is not only global but urgent in the extreme.

"Leaving aside generalized and ineffectual condemnations, pleas for more censorship or repressive legislation (these, in my view, can only exacerbate the situation or, at best, provide only a temporary palliative), and resisting the temptation to ignore the whole issue, what practical and positive steps can we take to produce that 'more discriminating public' . . .?"

A.W. Hodgkinson,
Screen Education

intents and purposes are purely avocational, not vocational. It is learning that applies to one's leisure activities, not to making a living. As our leisure time increases, more and more of it is filled with the mass media and popular culture, and as goes the audience, so goes the masspop.

As I see it, it is not simply a matter of "teaching movies" or "teaching television" but rather an opportunity to "teach life" by using the media as catalysts, as a means of bringing together interrelated knowledge and information from the total environment in an effort to "increase awareness of our common humanity and individual uniqueness," as A.W. Hodgkinson so artfully puts it.

THE PICTURE SHOWS:
an incomplete
bibliography

on films & movies

Daniel Talbot (ed.), **Film: An Anthology** (University of California Press)

W.R. Robinson (ed.), **Man and the Movies** (Pelican Books)

Richard Dyer MacCann (ed.), **Film: A Montage of Theories** (Dutton)

Joseph Gelmis, **The Film Director as Superstar** (Doubleday)

Kenneth Macgowan, **Behind the Screen** (Delta)

National Society of Film Critics, **Film 67/68, Film 68/69,** etc.
(Simon & Schuster)

Stanley Kauffmann, **A World On Film** (Delta)

Pauline Kael,
I Lost It At The Movies,
Kiss Kiss Bang Bang (Little, Brown, & Co./Bantam)
Going Steady (Little, Brown)

Judith Crist,
The Private Eye, The Cowboy, and The Very Naked Girl (Holt, Rinehart, & Winston/Popular Library)

Richard Schickel,
The Disney Version (Simon & Schuster/Avon)

Jerome Agel (ed.),
The Making of Kubrick's 2001 (Signet)

screenplays

Peter Fonda,
Dennis Hopper, Terry Southern,
Easy Rider (Signet)

William Goldman,
Butch Cassidy and The Sundance Kid (Bantam)

Horace McCoy &
Robert & Thompson, **They Shoot Horses, Don't They?** (novel & screenplay/Avon)

D.A. Pennebaker,
Bob Dylan: Don't Look Back
(documentary/Ballantine)

on the tube

Michael J. Arlen, **The Living Room War** (Viking)

Charles Sopkin,
Seven Glorious Days, Seven Fun-Filled Nights (Simon & Schuster/Ace)

Mason Williams,
The Mason Williams F.C.C. Rapport (Liveright)

Harlan Ellison, **The Glass Teat** (Ace)

Merle Miller & Evan Rhodes, **Only You, Dick Daring** (William Sloane Associates/Bantam)

Nicholas Johnson,
How To Talk Back To Your Television Set (Little, Brown, & Co./Bantam)

Fred Friendly,
Due To Circumstances Beyond Our Control (Random House)

Newton Minow, **Equal Time** (Atheneum)

on the school & the screen

John M. Culkin, S.J.,
Film Study in the High School (Fordham University)

A.W. Hodgkinson, **Screen Education** (UNESCO)

David Mallery,
The School and The Art of Motion Pictures (National Association of Independent Schools)

Sharon Feyen & Donald Wigal (ed.), **Screen Experience: an Approach to Film** (Geo. A. Pflaum)

David C. Stewart (ed.), **Film Study in Higher Education** (American Council on Education)

David A. Sohn,
Film Study and The English Teacher (Indiana University)

periodicals

Sight and Sound
(British Film Institute; London)

Cinema
(Spectator International, Inc.; Beverly Hills, California)

Media & Methods
(North American Publishing Co.; Philadelphia, Pa.)

See
(Screen Educators' Society, Inc., Chicago.)

. . . and THE AMERICAN FILM INSTITUTE Education Membership (1815 H Street NW; Washington, D.C.)

COLUMBIA DIS

THE AM/FM AND LP

Farrell North lives in my apartment building. He is twenty years old. For a living, he makes cabinets. He also makes woodcarvings, leathercraft, and very nice music on the guitar.

When Farrell was in 8th grade, he got an electric guitar from Montgomery Ward. By the time he was in high school, he had a Fender guitar and played in a rock 'n' roll band, knockin' 'em out with "Tears On My Pillow." Before he was out of high school, he had traded off the Fender and rock for an acoustic Gibson twelve-string and folk music.

Farrell hung around a Kansas City coffee house, learning how to play. He went to college, where he studied Urban Affairs for two years until he dropped out. The college, he says, wanted him to work toward a degree; he wanted to learn about what interested him and play music.

After he dropped out, he played music, and with an older brother, he started promoting pop concerts. Some financial setbacks, culminating in an ill-fated college concert the same week as the Kent State shootings (no one felt much like listening to music), put him out of business.

"Almost the only thing that I can give
other people is songs, and the rest is mine . . ."
—James Taylor

Farrell came west with his wife, Bonnie,
became a cabinetmaker, and began slowly to
recoup his losses and pay off his debts.
All the while, he practiced his guitar, wrote
his songs, and got ready to have another
go at it.

By this time next year, he hopes to be
playing music for a living again. By this time
next year, Farrell North might be a superstar
or just another itinerant folksinger on the
college concert/coffee house circuit or even
a cabinetmaker again. He says he has no
ambitions to be a star. Just playing music is
enough. He says he sees it as a "communication
trip"—singing about things that need to
be said. He really believes that music can
change things.

And there are hundreds, maybe thousands,
of Farrell Norths wandering around these
days . . .

"It's got a good beat, and you can dance to it."

—Teenagers' criteria for the critical evaluation of the rock 'n' roll (circa 1950s)

fifteen years of rock 'n' roll

Music is the major mass medium of the young today. It is the new electric lyric. More than any other medium, music is the tie that binds the counter culture. Like the other media, it is the shared experience of a generation. Many of us can measure our lives by popular music, can conjure up a "golden oldie" gestalt of other times, other places, other people, simply by hearing a song.

the first five: "Oldies But Goodies"

Until the mid-50s, they called it "rhythm & blues," and it was the black man's music, a segregated sound. Then came a movie called THE BLACKBOARD JUNGLE (ironies everywhere), and as the titles came on the screen, we heard:

"One-two-three o'clock,
  four o'clock, ROCK!
Five-six-seven o'clock,
  eight o'clock ROCK!
Nine-ten-eleven o'clock,
  twelve o'clock, ROCK!
We're gonna ROCK AROUND THE CLOCK
  TONIGHT!"

And when everyone had forgotten Glenn Ford as the tormented teacher and Sidney Poitier and Vic Morrow as the tough kids, they still remembered Bill Haley & The Comets and the coming of rock 'n' roll.

"Then, one Saturday night early in 1956 on a television variety program, a white singer drawls at the camera: 'Ladies and gentlemen, I'd like to do a song now, that tells a little story, that really makes a lot of sense—Awopbopaloobop—alopbamboom! Tutti-frutti! All rootie! Tootie-frutti! All rootie!'"

—Stanley Booth describes Elvis Presley in "A Hound Dog To The Manor Born"

"I think that Elvis is the cutest guy in the whole world."

—Roxie DeHerrera, age 16

Parents couldn't bear the volume. Forces for Good in the Community warned against implicit immorality in the funky Freudian banalities about teenage love. Pop music reviewers unanimously abhorred its crudity and advocated a return to Patti Page and Snookie Lansen. Nobody liked it but the kids, so it was bound to be a hit.

Out of Tupelo, Mississippi, came a kid by the name of Elvis Aaron Presley to become to music what Marlon Brando and James Dean were to movies. He played a kind of country blues with a rock 'n' roll beat, and he played with his whole body. Elvis Presley was to put some pazazz into an otherwise colorless time. Nobody but the kids liked him either. In fact, they didn't like him so much that he quickly became the biggest hit of all. In his book, **Woodstock Nation,** Abbie Hoffman says the Revolution started when Ed Sullivan refused to show Elvis Presley from the waist down. Could be.

The Forces for Good in the Community tried to give us the cleanliness and decency of Pat Boone and white buck shoes as a substitute for the raunchiness of Presley and long, bushy sideburns; but the '50s were already overloaded with Pat Boones and nobody **really** bought it.

"Rock music is a necessary element of
contemporary society. It is functional.
It is healthy and valid artistically. It is also
educational (how to ask a girl for a date,
what love is like). It has all the answers to
what your mother and father won't tell you.
It is also a big business."

—Frank Zappa

We wore our levis low and our collars up, and we watched Sal Mineo movies and the televised sock-hops of Dick Clark's AMERICAN BANDSTAND. We cruised the drive-ins in a '49 Ford with fuzzy dice or a rubber shrunken head hanging from the rear-view mirror. The radio played Fats Domino, Paul Anka, Little Richard, Buddy Holly, Chuck Berry, The Everly Brothers, The Drifters, The Coaster, et al. We never thought about Korea or President Eisenhower or anything much outside of high school. We hardly ever thought at all.

the second five: Pickin' & Strummin; Poetry & Politics

In college, in the early '60s, one abandoned rock 'n' roll for the sake of sophistication. Instead of Elvis Presley, we listened to Miles Davis, Dave Brubeck, the MJQ. Jazz was beginning to feel the cultural embrace, and its musicians were becoming artists instead of entertainers. Pop culturally, we were trapped between a juvenile rock 'n' roll about high school and hot rods or cycles and surfboards, and a progressive jazz which often demanded extensive music-theory prerequisites to be properly appreciated.

Into the breach came three jolly joe-college boys who called themselves The Kingston Trio. They sang a pepped-up kind of folk music that gave the folk purists fits.

"We don't really consider ourselves
folk-singers in the accepted sense
of the word . . ."

—Dave Guard of The Kingston Trio

The trio's instrumental abilities suggested "Play Guitar in Seven Days or Your Money Back" magazine ads, but for all their inadequacies as "folk singers" their frat house harmonies and talent show gusto still struck a responsive chord. Like rock 'n' roll, and unlike jazz, this was a do-it-yourself music, and in no time at all, everybody did.

Get yourself a guitar. Learn a half-dozen basic chords. Check out the Alan Lomax books from the college library, and—presto!—instant folksinger. Find a bass player and a banjo picker. Tune together, and—presto!—instant folk group. Many were called but few were chosen. The ersatz Kingston Trios went forth from the campuses and the coffee houses. They got bigger (The New Christy Minstrels, The Back Porch Majority) and better (The Limelighters, Bud & Travis, The Chad Mitchell Trio, Peter, Paul & Mary). And folk music became the new market to be milked dry by the mass media. Record companies gave us fast-buck groups that made The Kingston Trio sound like the original Weavers. Television gave us HOOTENANNY—folksy AMERICAN BANDSTAND. The movies even gave us TOM DOOLEY, based on the ballad, starring Michael Landon (who was to go on to such other starring roles as the lead in I WAS A TEENAGE WEREWOLF and Little Joe on TV's BONANZA).

"a song is anything that can walk by itself
i am called a songwriter.
a poem is a naked person . . .
some people say that i am a poet."

—Bob Dylan, liner notes for
BRINGING IT ALL
BACK HOME

The fate of folk music seemed to be sealed.

Then, out of Hibbing, Minnesota, came young Bob Dylan (nee Zimmerman), certainly the most unlikely candidate for superstardom ever to ramble down that ol' hot, dusty road. Dylan's voice was raspy. His guitar work was rustic. His songs were raw and real.

Despite the marked differences between Dylan and the ivy league pop folkies of the day, it was probably not uniqueness that was to make Dylan a demigod, but rather his ordinariness.

Dylan, if we were to believe his biography, had done what many of us had secretly wanted to do. Like Jack Kerouac, Dylan had gone "on the road," dropping out of college to learn about life first-hand. Dylan emulated the idolized Woody Guthrie, whose dustbowl ballads were legend and common to the repertoire of every would-be folksinger in the country. Dylan's own songs dramatized the issues that concerned us all—civil rights, the Bomb, social injustice. His love songs were about backstreet bedrooms and bittersweet farewells, not moon and June and high school rings. Bob Dylan was much more than a mere folksinger. He was a humorist, philosopher, social critic, poet, prophet, and lover. He was a beatnik, outlaw, underdog, cowboy, hobo, and hero. In his sheepskin jacket, buckskin boots, faded

"To sing is to love and to affirm, to fly and
soar, to coast into the hearts of the people
who listen, to tell them that life is to live,
that love is there, that nothing is a promise,
but that beauty exists and must be hunted for
and found. That death is a luxury, better to
be romanticized and sung about than dwelt upon
in the face of life."

—Joan Baez, **Daybreak**

jeans, and Sears & Roebuck work shirt, he
was the New American Youth Myth incarnate.

Along with Dylan, another influential force
in popular folk music was a gentle young
lady from Palo Alto, California. Her name
was Joan Baez, and her appearance met with
enthusiasm from purists and pop fans alike.
Her early repertoire was composed exclusively
of traditional material—Child ballads and
authentic early American songs, sung in a pure
ethereal soprano voice that brought raves
from music critics and rising record sales from
the audience. But Joan Baez did not cater to the
commercial whims of show business. Like Dylan,
she went her own way, at her "own chosen
speed." Turned on by Dylan's songs, she began
to incorporate new material into her traditional
repertoire with increasing emphasis on what was
termed the "social protest" song. Joan Baez'
idealism and social conscience soon became
her hallmark, not a fictitous promotional "image,"
but rather a sincere, heartfelt dedication to an
ethos of love, peace, and non-violence, which
was to become the banner (if not always the
practiced belief) of those involved in the
ensuing youth movement she helped to create.

Baez and Dylan opened the doors for what
Richard Farina called "a generation singing out."
New singer-songwriters appeared to add
momentum to the "folk

"The students, seeking a more profound language and finding such language in folk music, looked to folk musicians as their spokesmen."

—Richard Farina, "Baez and Dylan: A Generation Singing Out" in **Long Time Coming And A Long Time Gone** music revival." For the most part, they were not imitative replicas of the prototypes, as one might expect from a music industry infamous for its carbon copies, but were more often honest young musicians with original contributions to make to the the new American musical experience.

From Oklahoma came Tom Paxton. From Ohio, Phil Ochs. From New York, Eric Andersen. From Colorado, Judy Collins. From Massachusetts, Buffy Sainte-Marie. From Georgia, Patrick Sky. From New Hampshire, Tom Rush. From Florida, Fred Neil. From Canada, Gordon Lightfoot and Ian and Sylvia Tyson. From anywhere and everywhere, many many more.

New York City's Greenwich Village became the crossroads of the new music. There, in the bars and coffeehouses, in Washington Square or at Israel Young's Folklore Center, the new musicians came together to share songs and stories and instrumental styles.

Their works were etched on black vinyl, sold for four dollars an album, and the ideas set to music were sent out to the stereos of America.

The market label—"Folk Music"—stuck, even as the music drifted more and more toward original material and contemporary themes. Even Pete Seeger, America's foremost folksinger, began to sing the new songs along with his folk classics.

"A good song is like a many-faceted jewel.
Or a woman of many moods.
Or a tool of many uses . . .
It takes singers to bring them to life.
And such is their magic, that they can
bring fuller life to you."

—Pete Seeger, introduction to
America's Favorite Ballads

It must be folk music indeed, for folk music, by definition, is music "originated or used among the common people." There is no small print that says it cannot be

a) less than a hundred years old,
b) heard on the radio and records,
c) very popular.

What we hear now and what we will be hearing in the future is surely the "folk music" of the 20th century, for never before have so many folk been tuned in to the same songs.

the third five: Plugging In & Turning On

Berkeley, 1965: The Bob Dylan Concert. In the audience—Allen Ginsberg, beat poet in transition to hippie guru; Ken Kesey, the new Kerouac; Joan Baez; and the University of California students who are beginning some student power and anti-war activities which will set a style for national and international revolts in academia. Dylan does the first half of the concert solo, singing the familiar songs. Then, for the second half, he brings on his back-up band, straps on his electric guitar, and plays his own new brand of rock 'n' roll. Rock? Dylan? At first, it seems to be a contradiction in terms. For "selling out" like this, Dylan had been heartily booed earlier at the Newport Folk Festival and at his concert in Forest Hills, New York. But in Berkeley, nobody booed. They loved it.

"A guitar's all right, John, but you'll never earn your living by it."

—John Lennon's aunt, 1956

"What do you think of Beethoven?"
"I love him," said Ringo.
"Especially the poems."

—from **The Beatles: The Authorized Biography** by Hunter Davies

Big Sur, 1965: The Big Sur Folk Festival. On the evening prior to the festival, Joan Baez, critic Ralph Gleason, and other participants hold a panel discussion concerning the effect of rock on folk music. The discussion is frequently sidetracked into talk of peace and politics but much mention is made of a popular new English quartet called The Beatles.

The Beatles were to rock 'n' roll what Dylan was to folk, what Elvis Presley was to an earlier era. Although they were English, their music, at first, was basically American '50s boy-meets-girl, or boy-loses-girl, or boy-gets-girl, etc., distinguished by some elusive quality over and above the fact that it "had a good beat and you could dance to it." In the midst of a lot of serious social protest, perhaps the Beatles' initial success can be attributed to the fact that their happy music with a heavy beat provided relief and release from the increasing tensions of the time.

But the Beatles, like Baez and Dylan, refused to conform to a commercial image. By 1965, their changes were already reflected in their music, and would-be imitators began to fall by the wayside in their desperate efforts to keep up. In the course of their career, The Beatles evolved from teenybopper idols to Mack Sennett-style screen comedians, to archetypal hippies, to transcendental

"This generation is producing poets who write songs, and never before in the sixty-year history of American popular music has this been true."

—Ralph J. Gleason, liner notes for the Simon & Garfunkel album, PARSLEY, SAGE, ROSEMARY AND THYME mystics, to music business entrepreneurs, without breaking stride. Each of the Beatles retained and exhibited an individualistic personality, outlook, and life style, and along with the music, "Beatlemania" offered four distinct role models for the fans.

In the wake of the Beatles, the record industry laid on a barrage of hirsute British bands. Disregarding those that were nothing more than bogus Beatles, England exported the Anglo-honky blues of the Rolling Stones, the Yardbirds, Manfred Mann, John Mayall and Eric Clapton. They also sent over a second-string Scottish Dylan named Donovan, an explosive expatriate black American named Jimi Hendrix, a self-destructive group called The Who, a supergroup called Cream, and Procol Harum, and Traffic, and Pentangle, and the Moody Blues, and the Fairport Convention, and the Hollies, and Jethro Tull, and Joe Cocker, and . . . . .

In the U.S.A. during the last half of the '60s, ex-folksingers everywhere were plugging in, and creating new sounds faster than the trade papers could come up with labels. Paul Simon, of Simon & Garfunkel, wrote songs about alienation, man's inhumanity to man, and all those themes that had previously been associated with literature classes. John Sebastian and his Lovin' Spoonful gave us a funky-jugband-rock 'n' roll that they called "good-time music." John Phillips' Mamas

"If You Go To San Francisco
(Be Sure To Wear Flowers In Your Hair)"

—title of the Haight-Asbury
anthem written by John
Phillips, recorded by
Scott McKenzie, taken to
heart by thousands of young
pilgrims

Putting it in perspective, it is more probable that, throughout the country, more people were turning on to the music by itself than were tripping to it with the aid of chemistry. It seems highly doubtful that the millions of albums by the new rock bands were all bought by hard-core drug addicts.

The music of the Jefferson Airplane, the blues of Janis Joplin and Big Brother & The Holding Company, the psychedelic jams of Jerry Garcia and The Grateful Dead, the Berkeley balladry of Country Joe & The Fish, are all interesting and exciting musical experiences in their own right, even taken straight.

The climax and culmination of the new American musical experience came about in upstate New York in 1969. The Woodstock Music and Art Fair brought nearly half-a-million people together to see Baez, The Band, Blood, Sweat & Tears. Paul Butterfield, the Creedence Clearwater Revival, Crosby, Stills, Nash & Young, the Dead, Arlo Guthrie, Tim Hardin, Richie Havens, Hendrix, the Incredible String Band, the Airplane, Joplin, Melanie, Mountain, Santana, Sebastian, Ravi Shankar, Sly & The Family Stone, The Who, and one another.

Like all pop phenomena, the subculture revolving around rock has created its own mythology, and the myth of rock has been celebrated in song and print and on film and television as to the

"If the name 'Woodstock' has come to denote the flowering of one phase of the youth culture, Altamont has come to mean the end of it."

—Ralph J. Gleason, "Aquarius Wept" in **Esquire** (1970)

"three days of Love, Peace & Music" at Woodstock.

As recounted or implied in the "Woodstock Nation" Myth, American society is divisible into Good Guys and Bad Guys. The Good Guys have long hair. The Bad Guys have crew cuts. The Good Guys are the young underdogs. The Bad Guys are the old Establishment, the System, the Power Structure, the overdogs—corrupt, oppressive, and maniacally materialistic. The Good Guys, being more humanistic and idealistic, are confronted with the limited options of dropping out (into the Revolution or the "Alternative Society"), or selling out (going straight, giving in). As with any myth, there are some elements of truth, albeit exaggerated, in the Woodstock youth myth.

That which was sham and illusion in the myth was dramatically dispelled a few months after Woodstock at an isolated drag strip in Northern California. The place was Altamont. The star performers were the Rolling Stones.

Altamont was to Woodstock as the Rolling Stones were to the Beatles, as Hell's Angels were to flower children, as realism is to romanticism, as hate is to love. The Rolling Stones' hour had come around. Their image was that of the street gang in Anthony Burgess' **A Clockwork Orange.** The Stones weren't ones to sing of love, peace, and joy. Their songs were hard, dirty blues about sex and violence and fighting in the streets. For five years, they had been

"Altamont changed a lot of people's heads . . ."
—advertisement for the
Maysles Brothers'
documentary film
GIMME SHELTER.

waiting in the wings, powerful and popular performers, but always slightly out of fashion—bad vibrations in the midst of good karma. But the times were still a-changing. Non-violent dissent seemed ineffectual. The Vietnam war went on. Political tokenism had made no substantial changes in the ghettoes. Paranoia and polarization were rampant—Good Guys vs. Bad Guys. The radical elements of the New Left were calling for action, abandoning debate. Maybe Mick Jagger and the Rolling Stones had the answer . . .

People got killed at Altamont. One of them was stabbed and beaten to death by a Hell's Angel. The Angels, supposedly converted to hippiedom by Ken Kesey and his Merry Pranksters, had been hired by the Stones to keep order at Altamont. They kept it by beating people away from the stage with pool sticks. It soon became clear that the Hell's Angels, formerly the palace guard of the Golden Gate Park Be-Ins, could be as brutally piggish as any Chicago cop.

Altamont became the first Rock Horror Show, the "counter-Woodstock," the end of the myth, and the end of the '60s.

In the final analysis, the new music and its young audience are not accurately represented by either Woodstock or Altamont. Pop music **is** a "communication trip"—a medium with a multitude of messages, and, as Woodstock promoter Mike Lang pointed out, to understand young people is to understand their music.

"ah but in such an ugly time
the true protest is beauty . . ."
—Phil Ochs, protest singer

the next five: toward a synthesis in the '70s

The arbitrary categories of rock have never really existed as separate entities. They influence and are influenced by one another as well as by a wide variety of other sources.

As noted, for instance, the roots of rock are in rhythm and blues, and the contributions of "soul music" to the mainstream of rock and pop are endless. Without a doubt, the patterns of influence have been black on white more often than the reverse, and any comprehensive report on American pop music would have to rank the artistry of Otis Redding or Aretha Franklin right alongside that of Bob Dylan and Joan Baez.

In the '60s, the Motown sound was as widespread as that of the English imports, and, in fact, many of the English bands were heavily indebted to black musicians like Chuck Berry, Muddy Waters, Bo Diddley, and B.B. King, to name a few.

No folk or rock or folk-rock singer is unaware of the work of Leadbelly, Big Bill Broonzy, Josh White, Sonny Terry and Brownie McGhee, and Mississippi John Hurt, to name a few more. From Robert Johnson to Taj Mahal, from the Staple Singers to the Supremes, there is a wealth of music in the black heritage.

"I never thought that anyone would listen to my stuff in the same way that I listened to other people."

—Arlo Guthrie

The interest of the young in using music as a medium for personal statement and social comment has apparently afforded us a wellspring of fresh new talent and points of view, as exemplified in such singer-songwriters as Leonard Cohen, Joni Mitchell, James Taylor, John Stewart, Hoyt Axton, Jerry Jeff Walker, Tim Buckley, Harry Nilsson, Laura Nyro, Randy Newman, Kris Kristofferson, David Ackles, Carole King, and a great many more. In the abbreviated account of pop music given here—and considering the magnitude of the influx of poet-balladeers during the past few years—it is impossible to give each of them their due consideration. Again, this is a part of the task left to the initiative of the teacher and the students. Again, further investigation will be rewarded by many exciting discoveries.

In fifteen years, rock music has become virtually ubiquitous. The Aquarian musical, HAIR, brought rock to the theatre. Rock has become the theme music of many of the new movies, and appears as a frequent featured guest on television. For several years, it has been the prime content of radio (more about that momentarily). It has even been blessed with the cultural approval of Leonard Bernstein. In the prophetic '50s phrase of Danny & The Juniors, it would seem that "Rock and Roll is Here to Stay."

Like film, pop music is undergoing a period of growth and change, exploration and

"The Singapore government has forbidden the
sale or broadcast of the musical score of
the play 'Hair' and all records by the Beatles
in a campaign to suppress what the government
calls harmful Western influence . . .

"A radio-station spokesman said the Singapore
Ministry of Culture has decreed the banning
of 'drug-oriented and anti-establishment'
songs in particular."

—news story (UPI)

development. Aspects of all music are being assimilated. The Beatles and other groups became intrigued with the classical forms and instruments of Indian music, and made a pop star of sitarist Ravi Shankar (which is rather like making a pop star of Pablo Casals). Blood, Sweat & Tears and other groups incorporated jazz and rock in a manner acceptable to fans of both forms. Folk music, country & western music, and classical music have all provided inspiration for the synthesis of musical forms which is likely to be the pop of the '70s.

It also seems safe to speculate that the pop of the '70s, following new precedents, will continue to reflect the social context in which it is created.

At this writing, Elvis Presley is entertaining the older teenyboppers in Las Vegas. Bob Dylan continues to hide out, emerging occasionally to add another new chapter to his musical autobiography. Joan Baez, whose husband has been imprisoned for draft resistance, presents concerts that are half music, half polemic. The Beatles have broken up and gone their separate ways. The pop culture awaits the next musical messiah . . .

rock & radio

The main media for the propagation of pop and rock are records and radio. The content of the medium of radio is the medium of records, supplemented by the monotonous

"I feel that radio has a lot to do with the formation of the teen-age mind, such as it is."

—James Simon Kunen, **The Strawberry Statement**

enthusiasm of the disc jockey who chants
his perpetual time and temperature mantra
in between records and commercials for
pimple creams, boutiques, and soft drinks.

The main variations on the AM radio are
the music formats, which usually consist
of easy listening stations (elevator muzak),
country & western stations ("Friends and
Neighbors" radio), soul stations ("Can Ya Dig It?"
radio), and pop-rock stations ("Topfortygolden-
oldieteenybopperbubblegum" radio).

As a rule, the kind of rock heard on the
radio is not to be confused with the kind
of rock herein described. Taken as examples
of the genre, at least 75% of radio rock
would indicate a regression from the '50s.
It is directed, by and large, at the junior-high-age
girl who still buys 45 r.p.m. records to play
on her portable phonograph.

"Programming" (as in computer) is the
essence of AM rock radio. No dead air—
"the hits just keep on coming!"—and the
commercials just keep on coming, too.
With computerized consistency, the station
"play lists" are played and replayed until
every song in the Top Forty has been
tortuously beaten to death to make way for
forty more from the "pick hits."

Like television, radio takes no chances,
for fear of endangering its advertising

"I've noticed that the radio medium is a tremendous airy goofball which anesthetizes everyone who listens."

—Kunen, **The Strawberry Statement**

revenue. Like television, radio is primarily
programmed by business interests which are
totally indifferent to the level of entertainment,
so long as it proves to be absolutely
inoffensive in terms of everything except
our sensibilities. Like television, radio
is, first and foremost, an electronic sales pitch.

Record company businessmen, who are also in
it for the money, are at least subject to
the pressures of supply and demand. Theirs
not to argue the musical aesthetics or
personal philosophies of the performers;
theirs but to ring up the cash registers
and count the coin. Records are to radio
as film is to television—the dictates of
the audience vs. the dictates of the admen.

The best of the new music often goes all
but unnoticed by radio, except in those
rare instances (e.g., The Beatles) when
avoidance on the part of the programmers
is absolutely impossible. Neither Dylan
nor Baez nor many of their proteges were
given any significant amount of air time,
even in their heyday, when they were
changing the whole course of American
pop music.

Anything more topical than unrequited high
school romance is given short shrift on the
air waves. Skeptics are invited to call
their local "All Request" radio station,
and ask for practically anything by Phil
Ochs, Tom Paxton, early Dylan, or late Baez.

"I'm curious about the motivation of the people whose 50,000-watt pump pours such crap into the already polluted air."

—Kunen, **The Strawberry Statement**

In several large metropolitan areas, counter-measures have been taken by independent, innovative FM stations, which have come to be called "underground" radio. These stations play a non-programmed variety of music, including rock, folk, blues, jazz, classical, and any other good things that come along. Announcers are usually soft-spoken and distinguished by discernible individual personalities and musical tastes (as is not the case with radio announcers as a rule). The ads are not accompanied by eardrum-shattering fanfare and shouting, but are instead delivered in a straightforward, conversational manner which makes them informative and unobtrusive. It is a nice alternative.

Such alternatives deserve some encouragement for it is the underground and listener-supported stations which maintain some small degree of creativity in Radio Free America.

The potential of radio, cast aside in the aftermath of film and television, has never been fully realized, much less exhausted. Radio, like any mass medium, needs only people who will use it creatively instead of commercially. According to the rules and regulations of the Federal Communications Commission, the air waves used by radio and TV are the property of "the people" (us, remember?).

"They (the kids) use radio as a background,
the aural pop for whatever kind of life they want
to imagine they're leading."

—Tom Wolfe,
The Kandy-Kolored Tangerine-Flake Streamline Baby

In the words of Mason Williams:

"Is what the people want
What the people get?

"Is what the people want
What the people need?

"Is what the people need
What the people get?

"I think what the people get
is neither what they want
nor what they need."

Radio could be more than a bad soundtrack
for everyday life. It should be more.
We should insist on it.

the school & the sound

The teacher is a disc jockey of ideas.

Over and above exposing kids to new ideas,
he is also expected to serve as a critic
and interpreter, someone who can make some
sense of the ideas, extract their meaning,
and put them in perspective.

It is a dangerous profession. Discussion
of the ideas inherent in the new music
is bound to lead to topics like politics and
morality, which have been astutely circumlocuted
in the classrooms of the public schools.
Be prepared for hassles.

The stopgap measures of sidestepping the
issues or oversimplifying them, on the

"Rock is its own open-ended category. Why try to constrict it with traditional 'educational' tags?

"Similarly, there is no reason to limit rock lyrics to English courses. In its natural habitat—at home, in jukeboxes, at dances, in the global village that is the transistor radio—rock asks, and sometimes tries to answer, all manner of questions. And it reflects a broad spectrum of attitudes, yearnings, fulfillments, fantasies. Rock can be personal or collective, apolitical or polemical. It can be banal or piercingly evocative."

—Nat Hentoff, introduction to
Rock Is Beautiful

assumption that the kids will learn what they need to know "when they're older," is no longer tenable. They are older already. They have come of age by living their lives in the global village. They have come of age by accumulating an enormous amount of vicarious experience. They have come of age through exposure to the media.

They have a lot of questions. They are looking for answers. And they need them now.

Teachers don't have all the answers any more than songwriters or filmmakers have all the answers. But, an honest answer here, an honest answer there . . . . Every little bit helps. In the end, each of us must put the puzzle together for himself, but we can all use "a little help from our friends."

To teach the new music, of course, you have to listen to it, and hear what it has to say. Practically every school has phonographs. We use them to play records of Dylan Thomas reading his poetry. We can use them to play records of Bob Dylan singing his. If you are already familiar with the new music, you will be surprised at the number of things your kids haven't heard (thanks to radio). You might also be surprised to find out that much of what they have heard, they haven't **really** heard.

"It's time we stop, children,
What's that sound?
Everybody look what's going' down."

—Stephen Stills, FOR WHAT IT'S WORTH recorded by The Buffalo Springfield

As in screen studies, it is always best to start with what your kids already know and like, and to work out from there. Again, attempting to impose your own value judgments instead of teaching is a cop-out. Value judgments are inevitable, but they should be discussed and debated, not finally defined and dictated.

In regard to the controversial questions which invariably arise, the only alternative is honesty. For example, the whole question of drugs in connection with rock, as mentioned earlier, is a question of vital concern to many kids, and a question which calls for immediate, honest discussion, not evasive answers. I have heard teachers attempt to terrify kids about drugs with propagandistic misinformation about the "chromosomal damage inflicted by marijuana," or the "addiction resultant from shooting LSD." Such well-intentioned but ill-informed scare tactics are both ludicrous and useless. The dangers of drugs are real enough, as any ex-addict or medical authority will tell you. They need not be exaggerated and enhanced in fearsome, fictitious fables.

Some rock singers have sung the praises of the drug experience, but in other pop songs, drugs have been dramatically denounced (e.g., Hoyt Axton's SNOWBLIND FRIEND, KINGSWOOD MANOR, or THE PUSHER, Tom Paxton's CINDY'S CRYIN', or Buffy Sainte-Marie's CODINE). Somehow, those songs are never mentioned by Forces for

"But do these lyrics really amount to art? Does Wordsworth speak to Donovan from the great beyond? Is John Lennon's wordplay truly Joycean? Is Bob Dylan the Walt Whitman of the juke-box? In a sense, assertions like these are the worst enemy of liberated rock. They enslave it with an artificial heritage. The great vitality of the pop revolution has been its liberation from such encumberances of form. Rock swings free, embracing chaos, and laughing at the notion that there could be anything more worth celebrating than the present.

—Richard Goldstein,
introduction to **The Poetry of Rock**

Good in the Community who expound on the evils of the drug theme in rock, quoting at length the ambiguous lyrics of Dylan's TAMBOURINE MAN or Lennon & McCartney's LUCY IN THE SKY WITH DIAMONDS.

My own experience indicates that there exists a broad spectrum of points-of-view on a wide variety of subjects in the new music, and it is mostly a matter of providing equal time for the divergent opinions. Comparison and contrast are always effective means of dealing with ideas, and the new music lends itself easily to that method. Its points-of-view are as many as its musicians.

In referring to the new music, the term "poetry" has been used frequently here and elsewhere. It is used, to some extent, as a figure of speech, for only a select few pop lyrics can stand alone as verse, independent of the music. The music serves to reinforce the mood of the lyric and the over-all effect of the song in much the same way that intonation and inflection color speech. The musical context of the song is important.

I have known teachers to try to teach rock lyrics as poetry by mimeographing lengthy librettos for students to read in class. That is not what the new music is all about. The rhythm, the

"Don't criticize what you can't understand."
—Bob Dylan, THE TIMES
THEY ARE A-CHANGIN'

melody, the harmonies, the instrumentation, and even the recording production techniques are all contributing factors to the meaning of the music, and cannot be ignored. To study the words without the music is to study the content without the form. The two are inseparable.

There seems to be a tendency among teachers who treat media at all, to apply the old critical criteria to the new forms of communication—to appraise films, for instance, in the same way one appraises a novel, or to appraise pop songs as one appraises poetry. The consequence of this error is an abundance of negative criticism, not necessarily because a film is bad as a film or because a pop song is bad as a song, but because the film is not a good novel or the song is not a good poem. One function of the Electric Humanities must be the development of new critical criteria for evaluating media experience and popular entertainment.

Teaching records and radio is a parallel to teaching film and television. The new music and the new movies are often noteworthy for the new ideas which they express. On the other hand, radio and television are noteworthy because of the profound **absence** of ideas which they exhibit. This lack can be largely attributed to the censorious sterilization of radio and TV by controlling sponsors.

The result of that sterilization is often a diminution of America, at home and

"You broadcasters are at the center of the national debate. You are in the eye of the hurricane.

"Your public trust is the obligation to move forward—here, now, today—to perfect this magnificent instrument of broadcasting. The public must have its say in your planning and your building. It must, because you are much more than an industry.

"For the nation, you are our theater, our concert hall, our newsroom, our stadium, our picture window to the world. You shape the national conscience, you guide our children and you have it in your hands and hearts to shape history. Am I guilty of asking too much of broadcasting? Or, are you guilty of asking too little?"

—Newton N. Minow, address to the National Association of Broadcasters, 1962, in **Equal Time** abroad, to an image of a mythological fantasy-land, populated by beautiful, mindless robots, acting out absurd charades in the name of "entertainment"—an image devoid not only of intelligence and humanity but of truth, wisdom, and wit as well.

How our society appears through the TV tube and how it sounds through a transistor radio are topics to be considered, again in terms of the American image, American realities, and the American dream. Continued conjecture about what the media might be doing to us and what we might do about it in return will provide many interesting hours of class conversation, and hopefully, eventual action on the part of tomorrow's audience.

THE AM/FM AND LP: an incompleat bibliography

Jonathan Eisen (ed.),
The Age of Rock
(Random House/Vintage)

Richard Goldstein,
The Poetry of Rock (Bantam)
Goldstein's Greatest Hits
(Prentice-Hall)

Jerry Hopkins, **The Rock Story** (Signet)

Nik Cohn,
Rock From The Beginning (Stein & Day/Pocket Books)

J Marks,
Rock and Other Four-Letter Words
(Bantam)

Paul Williams, **Outlaw Blues** (Dutton/Pocket Books)

John Gabree, **The World of Rock** (Fawcett)

Stephanie Spinner (ed.), **Rock is Beautiful** (Dell)

Greil Marcus, **Rock and Roll Will Stand** (Beacon)

Editors of **Rolling Stone, Woodstock** (Straight Arrow Publishers)

Hunter Davies, **The Beatles** (McGraw-Hill/Dell)

Ralph J. Gleason, **The Jefferson Airplane and The San Francisco Sound** (Ballantine)

Joan Baez, **Daybreak** (Dial Press/Avon)

D.A. Pennebaker, **Bob Dylan: Don't Look Back** (Ballantine)

films

Murray Lener, FESTIVAL (Newport Folk Festival/1967)

D.A. Pennebaker, MONTEREY POP (Monterey Pop Festival/1967) BOB DYLAN: DON'T LOOK BACK (Dylan on tour/1967)

Michael Wadleigh, WOODSTOCK (1970)

The Beatles, LET IT BE (Beatles recording session/1970)

Christopher G. Knight, Robert Jones,
James Coyne, CARRY IT ON (documentary on Joan Baez/1970)

Maysles Brothers,
GIMME SHELTER (documentary on the Rolling Stones and Altamont)

an incompleat discography
(*The record albums included here were selected as a representative cross-section, and in accord with purely personal preferences)

ELVIS PRESLEY (RCA LPM 1254)

Frank Zappa & The Mothers of Invention,
CRUISIN' WITH RUBEN & THE JETS
(Verve/Bizarre V6-5055-X)

THE BEST OF THE KINGSTON TRIO
(Capitol/Star Line ST-1705)

THE BEST OF PETER, PAUL & MARY
(Warner Bros. 2552)

Bob Dylan,
THE TIMES THEY ARE A-CHANGIN'
(Columbia CL2105)
BLONDE ON BLONDE (Columbia C2S 841)
NASHVILLE SKYLINE (Columbia KCS 9825)
NEW MORNING (Columbia KC 30290)

Joan Baez,
JOAN BAEZ (Vanguard VSD 2077)
JOAN BAEZ/5 (Vanguard VSD 79160)
ONE DAY AT A TIME (Vanguard VSD 79310)
THE FIRST 10 YEARS (Vanguard VSD 6560/1)

Judy Collins, IN MY LIFE (Elektra EKS-74027)

Tom Rush, THE CIRCLE GAME
(Elektra EKS-74018)

Tom Paxton, TOM PAXTON/6
(Elektra EKS-74066)

Phil Ochs, PLEASURES OF THE HARBOR
(A&M SP4133)

Tim Buckley, GOODBYE AND HELLO
(Elektra EKS-7318)

Gordon Lightfoot,
SIT DOWN YOUNG STRANGER
(Reprise 6392)

Eric Andersen,
TODAY IS THE HIGHWAY (Vanguard
VSD 79157)

Buffy Sainte-Marie,
IT'S MY WAY! (Vanguard VSD
79142)

Leonard Cohen,
SONGS OF LEONARD COHEN (Columbia
CS 9533)

Tim Hardin,
SUITE FOR SUSAN MOORE (Columbia CS
9787)

Hoyt Axton, MY GRIFFIN IS GONE
(Columbia CS 9766)

FRED NEIL (Capitol ST 2665)

John Stewart, CALIFORNIA BLOODLINES
(Capitol ST 203)

James Taylor, SWEET BABY JAMES
(Warner Bros. 1843)

Joni Mitchell, LADIES OF THE CANYON
(Reprise 6376)

The Beatles,
MEET THE BEATLES (Capitol ST 2047)
REVOLVER (Capitol ST 2576)
"HEY JUDE" & Other Hits (Apple SW 385)

The Rolling Stones,
BIG HITS: HIGH TIDE AND GREEN
GRASS (London NP-1)
THEIR SATANIC MAJESTIES REQUEST
(London NPS-2)
BEGGAR'S BANQUET (London PS-539)

Jefferson Airplane,
SURREALISTIC PILLOW (RCA LSP
3766)

Big Brother & The Holding Company,
CHEAP THRILLS (Columbia KCS 9700)

Country Joe & The Fish,
GREATEST HITS (Vanguard 6545)

Grateful Dead, LIVE DEAD (Warner-Seven 1830)

Ray Charles, A MAN AND HIS SOUL
(ABC-590X)

Aretha Franklin,
I NEVER LOVED A MAN THE WAY I
LOVE YOU (Atlantic 8139)

Otis Redding/The Jimi Hendrix Experience,
HISTORICAL PERFORMANCES
RECORDED AT THE MONTEREY
INTERNATIONAL POP FESTIVAL
(Reprise 2029)

The Byrds, GREATEST HITS
(Columbia CS 9516)

Buffalo Springfield, RETROSPECTIVE
(ATCO SD-33-283)

THE BEST OF THE LOVIN' SPOONFUL
(Kama Sutra/MGM KLP8-8056)

The Mamas & Papas,
FAREWELL TO THE FIRST GOLDEN ERA
(Dunhill/abc 50025)

Simon & Garfunkel, BOOKENDS
(Columbia KCS 9529)

BLOOD, SWEAT & TEARS (Columbia CS 9720)

CROSBY, STILLS, & NASH (Atlantic SD 8229)

THE BAND (Capitol STAO-132)

The Who, TOMMY (A Rock Opera,
Decca DXSW 7205)

HAIR (Original Broadway Cast, RCA LSO-1150)

WOODSTOCK (Soundtrack, Cotillion SD3-500)

eclectic adj.
selecting or selected from various systems, doctrines, or sources.

humanities n.
the branches of learning concerned with human thought and relations; esp. literature, philosophy, etc.

—**Webster's New World Dictionary of The American Language**

GREAT MAN-
Hitler
ALEX. THE GREAT
KARL MARX- COMMIE

"We're taught a what-should-be culture . . . But if we were taught This Is What Is, I think we'd be less screwed up."

—Lenny Bruce

THE ECLECTIC HUMANITIES

Now is the time to teach the total environment.

A cultural selectivity on the part of education is an untenable anachronism in an era when the other education offers a bombardment of information and ideas to contradict and conflict with the limited views of life offered in the schools.

We have dealt too long and too exclusively with the world as we wish it would be, without due regard for the way it is. Education, like the other mass media, has created its own mythology—myths of history, myths of art, myths of reason, myths of moralism.

Whatever the specific subject we may teach within the scope of the arts and humanities, we are supposed to be teaching about life and ideas. Ideas can be approached by many more methods than we presently employ. Great works of art are expressions of ideas —ideas that determine the course of history, ideas on which entire cultures rise and fall. On another level, popular arts are also expressions of ideas—ideas that guide or change the course of individual lives (and thus determine social change), ideas that establish premises for personal perception of life and the world around us.

All ideas are the province of education. All ideas are interrelated. All ideas should be brought into the classroom.

"Where student interest is already focused is the natural point at which to be in the elucidation of other problems and interests. The educational task is not only to provide basic tools of perception but also to develop judgment and discrimination with ordinary social experience.

"Few students ever acquire skill in analysis of newspapers. Fewer have any ability to discuss a movie intelligently. To be articulate and discriminating about ordinary affairs and information is the mark of an educated man. It's misleading to suppose there's any basic difference between education and entertainment. This distinction merely relieves people of the responsibility of looking into the matter. It's like setting up a distinction between didactic and lyric poetry on the ground that one teaches, the other pleases. However, it's always been true that whatever pleases teaches more effectively."

—Marshall McLuhan,
"Classroom Without Walls"
in **Explorations in Communication**

If we give emphasis to certain ideas, excluding others, as we have in the past, we commit the same offense that we find objectionable in the mass media. We are then in no position to cast aspersions on the media for catering to a vague, undefined mass, if we are guilty of what amounts to the same thing: We are using education as a mass medium, directed at a "common denominator," without regard for any equal time provision to allow conflicting points-of-view. We are, in effect, censoring available ideas to serve our own purposes. Such tactics, however idealistic the motives, cannot be truly considered "education," defined as learning for living in the world as it is.

We have attempted, in our schools, to introduce students to the extraordinary experiences of art, while completely bypassing the ordinary experiences of their everyday lives. The school has always seen itself as the guardian-protector of America's children, sheltering them from the rude realities of life, and as the champion of "refinement" and "good taste." But for all those years of education, ours is not an especially refined society, and the rude realities are with us still.

We have not, in short, accomplished what we set out to do, which was to create a society of humanists who would apply the

"We have found out that art does not have to be difficult to be good. We have found out that the emotional impact of art does not have to be based on old sentiments and old profundities. And we are beginning to wonder if there is anything wrong with art which is popular, which is enjoyed by the massive middle-group of us who are not as informed or as experienced in factual sophistication as the tiny elite which used to be the guardian of all things artistic."

—J Marks, **Rock and Other Four-Letter Words: Music of The Electric Generation**

"Art is anything you can get away with."

—Marshall McLuhan

ideals perpetuated by art and culture in their everyday lives, thereby creating a new Utopia. It seemed like a good idea, but we blew it. We educated the young for Utopia, then thrust them out into a world which seldom measured up. The initial shock of "real life" often seemed to refute what they had learned, and often shattered expectations, bringing on an embittered denial of liberal arts education as wishful thinking, totally unrelated to the realities of the world.

Art and life become a dichotomy. Culture becomes the badge of an elite, a status symbol for the select few, instead of a source of joy and enlightenment for every man. Despite the educational exposure—or maybe because of it—the mass of men abandoned high culture, and set about creating a culture of their own—a culture which the elitist is quick to demean with words like "middle-brow," "plebian," "Phillistine," and "popular," a culture toward which the greater percentage of our students will eventually gravitate.

It is that culture, and its numerous sub-cultures, which the Electric Humanities proposes to investigate. To call for a study of popular culture is not to advocate a total reversal of the traditional educational approach by substituting the study of masspop for the study of art. What we need to achieve is a balanced study of both, not as separate entities, but as mutual reflections of the human

"The relation between high culture and popular culture seems to me filled with hopeful possibilities in spite of the fear, snobbery, and anti-intellectualism that now so often operate to inhibit easy movement between them."

—David Riesman, **The Lonely Crowd**

"There is a great need, I think, for a criticism of 'popular culture' which can acknowledge its pervasive and disturbing power without ceasing to be aware of the superior claims of the higher arts, and yet without a bad conscience."

—Robert Warshow, **The Immediate Experience**

"Trash has given us an appetite for art."

—Pauline Kael, **Going Steady**

condition. The Electric Humanities is but
a back-door approach to the same ideas
that provide the substance of a liberal
arts education.

It is time for us to do away with the
dictation of value judgments and to turn
our attention to that which proves educationally
valuable, whatever it may be, wherever it
can be found. It is time to start using that
which is available to us—the mass media,
the popular culture, the immediate experience,
as well as art—in our efforts to teach the
humanities. Several of these resources,
the most obvious, have been mentioned here,
but there is much, much more within the total
environment. All that is needed to make the
most of it is creative imagination, and a
willingness to explore and to innovate.

Teachers of the total environment must,
naturally, be generalists, who can draw
ideas from every area of experience.
The unfortunate tendency, in this age of
specialization, is merely to introduce yet
another specialty—Media Studies—instead of
applying the potential in a larger, more
comprehensive way. The Electric Humanities
intends to be to media studies as forestry is
to tree surgery.

The Electric Humanities can ideally function
as more than just another class. It should
function as a class directly related to all
other classes and to the world outside the
school as well.

"It is better to ask some of the questions
than to know all the answers."
—James Thurber

"The Answer is that the Answer changes."
—Mason Williams

"Questions are instruments of perception."
—Postman & Weingartner

Just as the program attempts to draw from all available ideas, it should also attempt to draw from all available sources in the school and outside. Generalist or not, no teacher can be a renaissance man today. There is too much to know. Therefore, the teacher should not hesitate to tap knowledgeable resource people—the kids, his colleagues, community professionals—whenever his own abilities to deal with a given subject are exhausted.

A part of the task is searching for answers. Another, even more important, part is asking the questions. The search for answers doesn't end with the last day of class, or with a high school diploma, or with a college degree. It is a lifelong business, and often the best we can do, as teachers, is to get it off to a good start. To ask the questions that are not easily answered—questions about the nature of man, about life and its meaning, about Truth or Beauty on Good—is what the humanities are for. In regard to those ends, the Electric Humanities is completely conventional.

In our burgeoning technocracy, there is a great need for the humanities if man's spirit is to keep pace with the power of his inventions. It is time we learned to use the tools of the technological environment to help create a humanitarian environment for the constructive employment of our tools.

"If there is any period one would desire to be born in,—is it not the age of Revolution; when the old and the new stand side by side, and admit of being compared; when the energies of all men are searched by fear and hope; when the historic glories of the old can be compensated by the rich possibilities of the new era? This time, like all times, is a very good one, if we but know what to do with it."

—Ralph Waldo Emerson, 1837

Ours is indeed a time of revolution—as are all times. Change is the constant. Only by accepting change and learning to live with it can we hope to prevail. It is time to teach the present and the future as well as the past. It is time to start building the "classroom without walls."

WHY?

"It may be said that we live in the world
of 'etc.' There is always more to start with
than we can take into account. There is always
more to say than we can possibly say. There is
always more to end with than we
can imagine . . ."

—Don Fabun, **Communications**

etc.

DON ALLEN received his B.A. degree in English from the University of Northern Colorado, and his M.A. in Mass Communications from the University of Denver. On the basis of his thesis, **The School & The Screen** (D.U., 1968), he received one of the first education fellowships awarded by the American Film Institute, and subsequently attended the A.F.I. Leadership Conference: On Teaching The Film, at the University of California, Santa Barbara, 1968.

Mr. Allen currently teaches the Electric Humanities at West High School in Denver, Colorado. He is a Pisces.

TOM PAXTON
JUDY COLLINS
BOB DYLAN

ent Warren - photographer designer - born 1946 - still alive - resides in denver, colorado -

CREDITS:

Quotations from **The Making of a Counter Culture** by Theodore Roszak, copyright ©1968, 1969, reprinted by permission of Doubleday & Company, Inc.

Quotations from **Explorations in Communication** edited by Marshall McLuhan & Edmund Carpenter, copyright ©1960 by the Beacon Press, reprinted by permission of Beacon Press.

Quotations from **The Medium is the Massage** by Marshall McLuhan & Quentin Fiore, copyright ©1967 by Marshall McLuhan, Quentin Fiore & Jerome Agel, published by Bantam Books, Inc., New York, reprinted by permission.

Quotations from **I Seem To Be A Verb** by R. Buckminster Fuller, copyright ©1970 by Bantam Books, Inc., used by permission.

Quotations from John M. Culkin reprinted by permission of the author.

Quotation from **Responsibility in Mass Communication** by William L. Rivers & Wilbur Schramm reprinted by permission of Harper & Row, Publishers, Inc.

Quotations from **The Effects of Mass Communication** by Joseph T. Klapper, copyright ©1960 by The Free Press, a Corporation, used by permission.

Quotations from **The Living Room War** by Michael J. Arlen used by permission of The Viking Press, Inc.

Quotations from **I Lost It At The Movies** and **Going Steady** by Pauline Kael reprinted by permission of Atlantic-Little, Brown & Company.

Quotation from **The Hidden Persuaders** by Vance Packard, copyright ©1957, reprinted by permission of David McKay Company, Inc.

Quotation from **Brave New World Revisited** by Aldous Huxley reprinted by permission of Harper & Row, Publishers, Inc.

Quotations from **Superman** and **Batman**, copyright ©1939 by Detective Comics, Inc.; renewed 1966 by National Periodical Publications, Inc., used by permission.

Quotation from **A World On Film** by
Stanley Kauffmann reprinted by
permission of Harper & Row
Publishers, Inc.

Quotation from "Television and News"
by Walter Cronkite and from
"The Lost Tribe of Television" by
Marya Mannes from **The Eighth Art,**
copyright © 1962 by CBS Television
Network, reprinted by permission
of Holt, Rinehart and Winston, Inc.

Quotation from F.C.C. Commissioner
Nicholas Johnson used by
permission of the author.

Quotation from **Seven Glorious Days,**
Seven Fun-Filled Nights by
Charles Sopkin, copyright © 1968
by Charles Sopkin, reprinted by
permission of Simon & Schuster.

Quotation from **America's Favorite**
Ballads by Pete Seeger,
copyright © 1961 by Oak
Publications, used by permission.
All rights reserved.

Quotations from **Esquire** Magazine
by Ralph Gleason (© 1970) and
Stanley Booth (© 1968) reprinted by
permission of **Esquire** Magazine.

Quotation from the Introduction by Richard Goldstein to **The Poetry of Rock,** edited by Richard Goldstein, copyright ©1968, 1969 by Richard Goldstein, used by permission of Bantam Books, Inc.

Quotation from **Equal Time, The Private Broadcaster and The Public Interest** by Newton N. Minow, copyright ©1964 by Newton N. Minow, reprinted by permission of Atheneum Publishers.

Quotation from **Rock And Other Four-Letter Words** by J Marks, copyright ©1968 by J Marks, reprinted by permission of Bantam Books, Inc.

Quotation from **Mass Entertainment** by Harold Mendelsohn, reprinted by permission of the author.

Quotation from **The Lonely Crowd,** Abridged Edition, by David Riesman with Nathan Glazer and Reuel Denney, copyright ©1950, 1953, 1961 by Yale University Press, reprinted by permission of Yale University Press.

Quotations from **The Immediate Experience** by Robert Warshow, published by Doubleday & Co., reprinted by permission of Mr. Paul Warshow.

Quotations from **Communications: The Transfer of Meaning** by Don Fabun, copyright ©1968 by the Kaiser Aluminum & Chemical Corporation, used by permission of the publisher, Glencoe Press, A Division of The Macmillan Company.

Quotation from **Daybreak** by Joan Baez. Copyright © 1966, 1968 by Joan Baez. Reprinted by permission of the publisher, The Dial Press.

Quotation from **The Great Comic Book Heroes** by Jules Feiffer. Copyright © 1965 by The Dial Press, Inc. Reprinted by permission of the publisher.

The author also wishes to express his appreciation for the use of the other brief quotations which appear throughout **The Electric Humanities.** Every attempt was made to give appropriate accreditation for all quoted material. Subject to notification, any inadvertent errors or omissions will be corrected in future editions.

Special thanks to United Artists, Embassy Pictures, Trans-Lux Pictures, Paramount Pictures, Warner Brothers Pictures, Metro-Goldwyn-Mayer and Columbia Pictures for the movie stills used in THE PICTURE SHOWS.